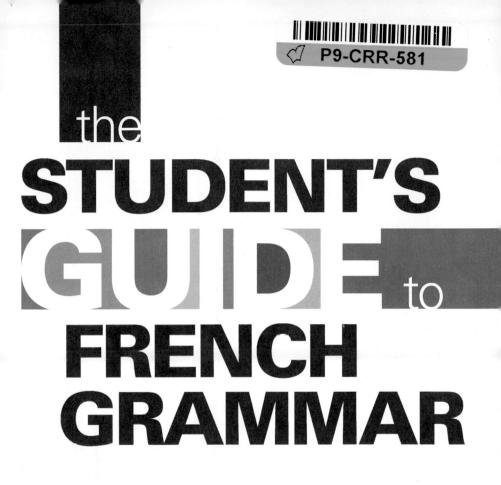

the
STUDENT'S
GUIDE
to
FRENCH
GRAMMAR

the
STUDENT'S
GUIDE to
FRENCH
GRAMMAR

Eric **Koseff**
Patrick **Karsenti**
Kwantlen Polytechnic University

Pearson Canada
Toronto

Library and Archives Canada Cataloguing in Publication
Koseff, Eric, 1965–
    The student's guide to French grammar / Eric Koseff, Patrick Karsenti.

Includes index.
ISBN 978-0-13-509406-8

    1. French language—Grammar—Textbooks. 2. French language—Textbooks for second
language learners—English speakers. I. Karsenti, Patrick II. Title.

PC2129.E5K68 2011   448.2'421   C2009-904822-1

ISBN 978-0-13-509406-8

Vice President, Editorial Director: Gary Bennett
Editor-in-Chief: Ky Pruesse
Senior Acquisitions Editor: Laura Pratt
Signing Representative: Carmen Batsford
Executive Marketing Manager: Judith Allen
Developmental Editor: Rema Celio
Managing Editor: Söğüt Y. Güleç
Copy Editor: Aude Lemoine
Proofreaders: Elaine Gareau, Vicki McDonald
Production Coordinator: Sarah Lukaweski
Composition: MPS Limited, A Macmillan Company
Art Director: Julia Hall
Cover and Interior Design: Anthony Leung

1 2 3 4 5   13 12 11 10 09

Printed and bound in USA.

To Tommy, Olive, Jenny, Jimmy and Tiger
—EK

Contents: Table des matières

During the course of my French teaching career, it became clear to me that my students needed brief, concise and informative data sheets to help them learn the language and understand grammatical structure. I therefore began to compile single-page information sheets that extract, explain and display the essence of a given topic of French grammar in a simple yet palatable manner. Once this was done, I felt that each and every student learning French would benefit from this format. Consequently, I proceeded to write this book.

I have colour-coded the book in order to highlight the elements that remain constant in the language (black) and those that need to be added, modified or emphasized (**purple**) for a given topic. For example, when conjugating a regular **ER** verb the colour-coding works as follows:

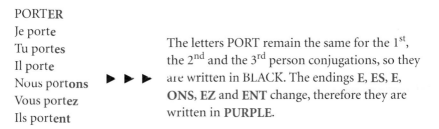

PORTER
Je porte
Tu portes
Il porte
Nous portons
Vous portez
Ils portent

The letters PORT remain the same for the 1st, the 2nd and the 3rd person conjugations, so they are written in BLACK. The endings **E**, **ES**, **E**, **ONS**, **EZ** and **ENT** change, therefore they are written in **PURPLE**.

A further example is that of the negative. The colour-coding demonstrates the position of the **NE** and **PAS**:

Ex.: Elle **ne** fait **pas** ses courses au supermarché.
     Vous **n'**avez **pas** assez de temps pour y aller.

Grammar textbooks tend to be long-winded, complicated and packed with exceptions. This is probably the most user-friendly grammar textbook you will ever come across. It is a manual that both teachers and students of all levels will find extremely useful and effective. The concise, colour-coded format makes French grammar easy, accessible and uncomplicated.

Supplements

CourseSmart for Instructors:

CourseSmart goes beyond traditional expectations—providing instant, online access to the textbooks and course materials you need at a lower cost for students. And even as students save money, you can save time and hassle with a digital eTextbook that allows you to search for the most relevant content at the very moment you need it. Whether it's evaluating textbooks or creating lecture notes to help students with difficult concepts, CourseSmart can make life a little easier. See how when you visit **www.coursesmart.com/instructors**.

CourseSmart for Students:

CourseSmart goes beyond traditional expectations—providing instant, online access to the textbooks and course materials you need at an average savings of 50%. With instant access from any computer and the ability to search your text, you'll find the content you need quickly, no matter where you are. And with online tools like highlighting and note-taking, you can save time and study efficiently. See all the benefits at **www.coursesmart.com/students**.

Acknowledgments

I would like to thank all the reviewers who contributed to this project:

Michel Acquarone
(George Brown College)

Alexandre Amprimoz
(Brock University)

Michael Bishop
(Dalhousie University)

Vadym Donsky
(York University)

Myriam Gosselin
(University of Alberta)

Christian Guilbault
(Simon Fraser University)

Annabelle Guillemain
(University of Alberta)

Jean Ntakirutimana
(Brock University)

Édouard Magessa O'Reilly
(Memorial University of Newfoundland)

Marilena Stalteri
(George Brown College)

Lynne Stewart
(University of Regina)

Milo Sweedler
(Wilfrid Laurier University)

Vina Triven-Gadum
(Athabasca University)

Bob Warren
(St. Lawrence College)

I would also like to thank the team at Pearson Canada: Laura Pratt (Senior Acquisitions Editor), Rema Celio (Developmental Editor), Söğüt Güleç (Managing Editor), Aude Lemoine (Copy Editor), Michel Acquarone (Subject Matter Expert), Elaine Gareau and Vicki McDonald (Proofreaders) and Christine Cozens (former Acquisitions Editor).

Finally, I would like to make special mention of Patrick Karsenti (Kwantlen Polytechnic University) for his invaluable contribution throughout the publishing process.

Eric Koseff

the
STUDENT'S
GUIDE to
FRENCH
GRAMMAR

Part 1 Verbs–Structure, Tenses and Moods: Verbes–structure, temps et modes

1a Subject Pronouns, Infinitive: Pronoms sujets, Infinitif

Subject Pronouns: Pronoms sujets

Definition: A SUBJECT PRONOUN refers to a person/thing and is the subject of a sentence.

JE	I
TU	YOU (informal, singular)
IL	HE
ELLE	SHE
ON	ONE/WE

NOUS	WE
VOUS	YOU (formal singular, or plural)
ILS	THEY (masculine)
ELLES	THEY (feminine)

There are two ways of saying YOU in French:

TU = YOU (singular) is used for informal interactions. **Ex.:** when speaking to a child, a friend, a fellow student or a member of the family.
VOUS = YOU (singular or plural) is used for formal interactions. **Ex.:** when speaking to a person you don't know well, a business associate or a person you meet for the first time. It is also used in the plural when speaking to many people in a formal or informal manner.

There are two types of THEY in French:

ILS = THEY (more than one male)
ELLES = THEY (more than one female)

NB | If a male is present in a group of females, then use the masculine **ILS**.

ON has several meanings:

ON = ONE
Ex.: **On** va en vacances en été. (One goes on holiday in the summer.)

ON = PEOPLE IN GENERAL
Ex.: En France, **on** parle français. This sentence can be translated in two ways: In France, people speak French. / In France, French is spoken.

ON = WE
Ex.: Ce soir, **on** va chez des amis. (This evening, we're going to friends.)

The use of **ON** as a substitute for **NOUS** is common practice in the French language.

Infinitive: Infinitif

Definition: A verb is a word that generally indicates an action and is the central element of a sentence. The most basic form or root of the verb is called the INFINITIVE. In English one can recognize the INFINITIVE form of the verb because it is almost always preceded by the word TO: to like, to succeed, to hear. In French the INFINITIVE is one word. The French language has three groups of verbs—ER, IR and RE VERBS. One can recognize the INFINITIVE form of the verb in French because the verb either ends in the letters ER, IR or RE. This is true for all infinitives in the French language.

ER	aimer	to like
IR	réussir	to succeed
RE	entendre	to hear

Each group of verbs—ER, IR and RE—have both REGULAR and IRREGULAR VERBS.

Some Useful Expressions That Are Followed by the Infinitive:

Je veux manger. (I want to eat.)	Je peux essayer. (I can try. / I am able to try.)
J'aime patiner. (I like to skate.)	Je dois partir. (I must leave. / I have to leave.)
Je souhaite sortir. (I wish to go out.)	Je déteste conduire. (I hate driving.)
Je désire commander. (I would like to order.)	J'ai envie de rester. (I feel like staying.)
J'ai besoin de travailler. (I need to work.)	Je viens de terminer. (I've just finished.)
Il faut commencer. (It is necessary to begin.)	Je suis en train de lire. (I'm busy reading.)

1b Present: Présent

Definition: The PRESENT TENSE indicates an action that takes place at this very moment.

Regular Verbs: Verbes réguliers

Definition: A REGULAR VERB is a verb that is conjugated in a fixed pattern.

Conjugating Regular ER, IR and RE Verbs

Start with the INFINITIVE, then drop the ER, IR or RE and ADD THE ENDINGS as shown below in PURPLE:

ER – Chanter (to sing)	IR – Finir (to finish)	RE – Vendre (to sell)
Je chante	Je finis	Je vends
Tu chantes	Tu finis	Tu vends
Il chante	Il finit	Il vend_
Elle chante	Elle finit	Elle vend_
On chante	On finit	On vend_
Nous chantons	Nous finissons	Nous vendons
Vous chantez	Vous finissez	Vous vendez
Ils chantent	Ils finissent	Ils vendent
Elles chantent	Elles finissent	Elles vendent

NB | Remember that in French there is only ONE present tense.
In other words, **je parle** can either mean "I speak" or "I am speaking" depending on the context.

NB | In the ILS and ELLES forms, the ending NT is not pronounced. Therefore, "il chante" and "ils **chantent**" sound exactly the same! But, "il **arrive**" and "ils_**arrivent**" will sound different because of the connection or liaison between the S and the A: "ils_arrivent."

Key Irregular Verbs: Verbes irréguliers-clés

The most important irregular verbs in the entire French language are ÊTRE, AVOIR and ALLER. Learn them well!

Être (to be)	Avoir (to have)	Aller (to go)
Je suis	J'ai	Je vais
Tu es	Tu as	Tu vas
Il est	Il a	Il va
Elle est	Elle a	Elle va
On est	On a	On va
Nous sommes	Nous avons	Nous allons
Vous êtes	Vous avez	Vous allez
Ils sont	Ils ont	Ils vont
Elles sont	Elles ont	Elles vont

The word EST means IS.

Être	C'est...	(It is . . .)
	Ce n'est pas...	(It is not . . .)
	Est-ce que...?	(Is it that. . . ?)
	Qu'est-ce que...?	(What is it that. . . ?)
Avoir	Il y a...	(There is/are . . .)
	Il n'y a pas...	(There isn't/aren't . . .)
	Il y a un mois...	(One month ago . . .)
Aller	Ça va?/Comment ça va?	(How's it going?)
	Comment allez-vous?	(How are you?)
	Comment vas-tu?	(How are you?) informal

1
b

1c Regular ER Verbs: Verbes réguliers en ER

Definition: The VERBS in the FIRST GROUP end in **ER**. In order to conjugate a regular **ER** verb, start with the INFINITIVE, then DROP the **ER** and add **E, ES, E, ONS, EZ, ENT**. Remember that the IL/ELLE/ON conjugations will always be the same. The same applies to ILS and ELLES. 80% of all **ER** verbs follow the regular pattern:

> **Demand er (to ask)**
> Je demand e
> Tu demand es
> Il/Elle/On demand e
> Nous demand ons
> Vous demand ez
> Ils/Elles demand ent

Regular ER Verbs

ador **er**	to adore	invit **er**	to invite
aid **er**	to help	jou **er**	to play
aim **er**	to like/to love	laiss **er**	to leave
apport **er**	to bring	lav **er**	to wash
arrêt **er**	to stop/to arrest	lou **er**	to rent
arriv **er**	to arrive	march **er**	to walk
attir **er**	to attract	mont **er**	to go up/
cach **er**	to hide		to get in (a car)
cass **er**	to break	montr **er**	to show
chant **er**	to sing	oubli **er**	to forget
cherch **er**	to look for	parl **er**	to speak
command **er**	to order	pass **er**	to spend (time)/
décid **er**	to decide		to pass
déjeun **er**	to have lunch	pens **er**	to think
demand **er**	to ask	port **er**	to carry/to wear
dérang **er**	to disturb	prépar **er**	to prepare

continued

continued

dîner	to have dinner	proposer	to suggest/
donner	to give		to propose
échapper	to escape	plaisanter	to joke
écouter	to listen	quitter	to leave
embrasser	to kiss	raconter	to tell
entrer	to enter	refuser	to refuse
étudier	to study	regarder	to look at/
expliquer	to explain		to watch
exprimer	to express	rencontrer	to meet
ennuyer	to bore	rester	to stay
envoyer	to send	retourner	to return/
essayer	to try		to go back
fumer	to smoke	tomber	to fall
fermer	to close	travailler	to work
gagner	to win/to earn	utiliser	to use
goûter	to taste	visiter	to visit
habiter	to live		

Some Slightly Irregular ER Verbs

acheter	→ j'achète, tu achètes, il achète, nous achetons, vous achetez, ils achètent.
appeler	→ j'appelle, tu appelles, il appelle, nous appelons, vous appelez, ils appellent.
payer	→ je paye/paie, tu payes/paies, il paye/paie, nous payons, vous payez, ils payent/paient.
jeter	→ je jette, tu jettes, il jette, nous jetons, vous jetez, ils jettent.
manger	→ nous mangeons.
commencer	→ nous commençons.

NB | **ALLER** is a HIGHLY IRREGULAR **ER** verb (see pages 5 and 12).

1d Regular IR Verbs: Verbes réguliers en IR

Definition: The VERBS in the SECOND GROUP end in **IR**. In order to conjugate a regular **IR** verb, start with the INFINITIVE, then DROP the **IR** and add **IS, IS, IT, ISSONS, ISSEZ, ISSENT**. 15% of all **IR** verbs follow the regular pattern:

> **Fin**ir **(to finish)**
> Je fin**is**
> Tu fin**is**
> Il/Elle/On fin**it**
> Nous fin**issons**
> Vous fin**issez**
> Ils/Elles fin**issent**

Regular **IR** Verbs

accompl**ir**	to accomplish	garant**ir**	to guarantee
alourd**ir**	to make heavy	guér**ir**	to cure/to heal/
anéant**ir**	to annihilate/		to recover
	to destroy	gross**ir**	to gain weight
approfond**ir**	to deepen	maigr**ir**	to lose weight
applaud**ir**	to applaud	meurtr**ir**	to bruise
agrand**ir**	to make larger	mun**ir**	to provide/
atterr**ir**	to land		to equip
attendr**ir**	to soften	obé**ir**	to obey
bât**ir**	to build	pun**ir**	to punish
blanch**ir**	to whiten	pâl**ir**	to go pale
bleu**ir**	to turn blue	ralent**ir**	to slow down
brun**ir**	to turn brown	réfléch**ir**	to think/to reflect
chois**ir**	to choose	rempl**ir**	to fill
défin**ir**	to define	réun**ir**	to reunite/to unite
démol**ir**	to demolish	réuss**ir**	to succeed

continued

continued

durcir	to harden	rougir	to blush
embellir	to embellish	raccourcir	to shorten
envahir	to invade	rajeunir	to rejuvenate
établir	to establish	saisir	to seize
enlaidir	to make ugly	salir	to dirty
élargir	to widen	subir	to suffer/
finir	to finish		to undergo
fournir	to supply	vieillir	to age/
grandir	to get bigger/		to grow old
	to grow up	verdir	to turn green

Some Irregular IR Verbs

(See pages 12, 13, 94 and 95.)

accueillir	to welcome	partir	to leave
avoir	to have	pouvoir	to be able to
couvrir	to cover	revenir	to come back
courir	to run	servir	to serve
concevoir	to conceive	sortir	to go out
devenir	to become	souffrir	to suffer
devoir	to have to/to owe	savoir	to know
dormir	to sleep	vouloir	to want
offrir	to offer/to give	venir	to come
ouvrir	to open	voir	to see

NB | Strangely enough, **offrir, ouvrir, couvrir** and **souffrir** are all conjugated like **ER** verbs: j'offre, tu offres, il offre, nous offrons, vous offrez, ils offrent.

1e Regular RE Verbs: Verbes réguliers en RE

Definition: The VERBS in the THIRD GROUP end in **RE**. In order to conjugate a regular **RE** verb, start with the INFINITIVE, then DROP the **RE** and add **S, S, _, ONS, EZ, ENT**. Five percent of all **RE** verbs follow the regular pattern:

Vendre (to sell)
Je vends
Tu vends
Il/Elle/On vend_
Nous vendons
Vous vendez
Ils/Elles vendent

Regular RE Verbs

attendre	to wait
défendre	to defend
dépendre	to depend
descendre	to go down/to descend
entendre	to hear
étendre	to spread out
fondre	to melt
mordre	to bite
pendre	to hang
perdre	to lose
prétendre	to claim
rendre	to give back
répandre	to spread
répondre	to answer
tendre	to tighten/to hold something out
vendre	to sell

Some Irregular RE Verbs

(See pages 12, 13, 94 and 95.)

apprendre	to learn
boire	to drink
connaître	to know
comprendre	to understand
corrompre	to corrupt
croire	to believe/to think
dire	to say/to tell
écrire	to write
être	to be
faire	to do
lire	to read
mettre	to put
prendre	to take
rompre	to break
suivre	to follow
vivre	to live

NB | When the verb begins with a vowel or a mute H, then the E of the "JE" falls away and becomes an apostrophe: j'aime, j'habite, j'applaudis, j'accomplis, j'entends.

BUT: tu aimes, tu arrives, tu habites AND elle aime, elle écoute, elle entend.

1
e

1f Useful Irregular Verbs: Verbes irréguliers utiles

Aller (to go)	Avoir (to have)	Boire (to drink)
Je vais	J'ai	Je bois
Tu vas	Tu as	Tu bois
Il/Elle/On va	Il/Elle/On a	Il/Elle/On boit
Nous allons	Nous avons	Nous buvons
Vous allez	Vous avez	Vous buvez
Ils/Elles vont	Ils/Elles ont	Ils/Elles boivent
Connaître (to know)	**Croire (to believe)**	**Devoir (to have to)**
Je connais	Je crois	Je dois
Tu connais	Tu crois	Tu dois
Il/Elle/On connaît	Il/Elle/On croit	Il/Elle/On doit
Nous connaissons	Nous croyons	Nous devons
Vous connaissez	Vous croyez	Vous devez
Ils/Elles connaissent	Ils/Elles croient	Ils/Elles doivent
Dire (to say/to tell)	**Dormir (to sleep)**	**Écrire (to write)**
Je dis	Je dors	J'écris
Tu dis	Tu dors	Tu écris
Il/Elle/On dit	Il/Elle/On dort	Il/Elle/On écrit
Nous disons	Nous dormons	Nous écrivons
Vous dites	Vous dormez	Vous écrivez
Ils/Elles disent	Ils/Elles dorment	Ils/Elles écrivent
Être (to be)	**Faire (to make/to do)**	**Lire (to read)**
Je suis	Je fais	Je lis
Tu es	Tu fais	Tu lis
Il/Elle/On est	Il/Elle/On fait	Il/Elle/On lit
Nous sommes	Nous faisons	Nous lisons
Vous êtes	Vous faites	Vous lisez
Ils/Elles sont	Ils/Elles font	Ils/Elles lisent
Mettre (to put)	**Ouvrir (to open)**	**Partir (to leave)**
Je mets	J'ouvre	Je pars
Tu mets	Tu ouvres	Tu pars
Il/Elle/On met	Il/Elle/On ouvre	Il/Elle/On part
Nous mettons	Nous ouvrons	Nous partons
Vous mettez	Vous ouvrez	Vous partez
Ils/Elles mettent	Ils/Elles ouvrent	Ils/Elles partent

Plaire (to please)	**Pouvoir (to be able)**	**Prendre (to take)**
Je plais	Je peux	Je prends
Tu plais	Tu peux	Tu prends
Il/Elle/On plaît	Il/Elle/On peut	Il/Elle/On prend
Nous plaisons	Nous pouvons	Nous prenons
Vous plaisez	Vous pouvez	Vous prenez
Ils/Elles plaisent	Ils/Elles peuvent	Ils/Elles prennent
Rire (to laugh)	**Savoir (to know)**	**Sortir (to go out)**
Je ris	Je sais	Je sors
Tu ris	Tu sais	Tu sors
Il/Elle/On rit	Il/Elle/On sait	Il/Elle/On sort
Nous rions	Nous savons	Nous sortons
Vous riez	Vous savez	Vous sortez
Ils/Elles rient	Ils/Elles savent	Ils/Elles sortent
Suivre (to follow)	**Tenir (to hold)**	**Venir (to come)**
Je suis	Je tiens	Je viens
Tu suis	Tu tiens	Tu viens
Il/Elle/On suit	Il/Elle/On tient	Il/Elle/On vient
Nous suivons	Nous tenons	Nous venons
Vous suivez	Vous tenez	Vous venez
Ils/Elles suivent	Ils/Elles tiennent	Ils/Elles viennent
Vivre (to live)	**Voir (to see)**	**Vouloir (to want)**
Je vis	Je vois	Je veux
Tu vis	Tu vois	Tu veux
Il/Elle/On vit	Il/Elle/On voit	Il/Elle/On veut
Nous vivons	Nous voyons	Nous voulons
Vous vivez	Vous voyez	Vous voulez
Ils/Elles vivent	Ils/Elles voient	Ils/Elles veulent

1
f

NB If you know how to conjugate **prendre** then you know how to conjugate com**prendre**, ap**prendre** and sur**prendre**. The same goes for **rire** and sou**rire**, **plaire** and dé**plaire**, **sortir** and res**sortir**.

NB In the VOUS form of the present tense, all verbs end in EZ except: vous ê**tes**, vous fai**tes**, vous di**tes**.
In the NOUS form, all verbs end in ONS except: nous **sommes**. In the ILS/ELLES form, all verbs end in ENT except: ils **sont**, ils **ont**, ils **vont**, ils **font**.
In the TU form, all verbs end in S except: tu veu**x**, tu peu**x**, tu vau**x**.

NB Some verbs only exist in the impersonal "il" form: Falloir → **il faut**, neiger → **il neige**, and pleuvoir → **il pleut**.

1g Reflexive Verbs: Verbes pronominaux

Definition: A REFLEXIVE VERB is a verb in which the subject performs the action on him/her/them or itself. All three groups of verbs—**ER**, **IR** and **RE**—have reflexive verbs. They can be regular or irregular. The infinitive of a reflexive verb always has **SE** or **S'** before the verb: se coucher, s'endormir, s'entendre. In order to conjugate a reflexive verb you have to add the REFLEXIVE PRONOUN to the conjugation: JE **ME**, TU **TE**, IL/ELLE/ON **SE**, NOUS **NOUS**, VOUS **VOUS**, ILS/ELLES **SE**. **Ex.:** je me lave (I wash myself), elle se demande (she wonders/she asks herself).

> **Se coucher (to go to bed)**
> Je **me** couche
> Tu **te** couches
> Il/Elle/On **se** couche
> Nous **nous** couchons
> Vous **vous** couchez
> Ils/Elles **se** couchent

1
g

Reflexive Verbs

s'amuser	to have fun
s'arrêter	to stop
s'appeler	to be called
se coucher	to go to bed
se débrouiller	to manage/to get by
se demander	to wonder
se démaquiller	to take makeup off
se dépêcher	to hurry
se déshabiller	to get undressed
s'endormir	to go to sleep/to fall asleep
s'ennuyer	to get bored
s'entendre (avec)	to get along (with)
se fâcher (contre)	to get angry (with)

continued

continued

s'habiller	to get dressed
s'intéresser (à)	to be interested (in)
se laver	to wash oneself
se lever	to get up
se maquiller	to put makeup on
se marier	to get married
se moquer (de)	to make fun (of)
s'occuper (de)	to take care (of)/to be busy (with)
se promener	to go for a walk
se rappeler	to remember
se raser	to shave
se rencontrer	to meet one another
se reposer	to rest
se retrouver	to meet up
se réveiller	to wake up
se sentir	to feel
se souvenir (dc)	to remember
se tromper	to be mistaken
se trouver	to be found/to be located

1
g

NB When the verb begins with a vowel or a mute H, then the E of the "ME", "TE" and "SE" falls away and becomes an apostrophe. Ex.: je m'habille, tu t'endors, il s'appelle, ils s'occupent de leurs enfants, elles s'entendent bien avec leurs parents, ils s'aiment beaucoup.

1h Near Future, Simple Future: Futur proche, Futur simple

Near Future: Futur proche

Definition: The NEAR FUTURE is used to describe what is going to happen. In order to form the NEAR FUTURE, conjugate ALLER in the PRESENT TENSE and add the INFINITIVE. Example: Je **vais** commenc**er** (I am going to begin).

PRONOUN/SUBJECT	ALLER IN THE PRESENT	INFINITIVE
Je	vais	essay**er**
Tu	vas	ven**ir**
Il	va	mang**er**
Elle	va	sort**ir**
On	va	demand**er**
Nous	allons	attend**re**
Vous	allez	comprend**re**
Ils	vont	décid**er**
Elles	vont	réuss**ir**

NB With a reflexive verb: je vais **me** coucher, tu vas **te** coucher, il va **se** coucher, nous allons **nous** coucher, vous allez **vous** coucher, ils vont **se** coucher.

Simple Future: Futur simple

Definition: The SIMPLE FUTURE is used to describe what will happen. In order to form the SIMPLE FUTURE, take the INFINITIVE form of the verb and ADD the **AVOIR** ENDINGS **AI, AS, A, ONS, EZ, ONT**. With **RE** verbs, the **E** of the infinitive falls away.

Example: Je répond**rai**. (I will answer.)

Rester	Partir	Répondre
Je resterai	Je partirai	Je répondrai
Tu resteras	Tu partiras	Tu répondras
Il restera	Il partira	Il répondra
Elle restera	Elle partira	Elle répondra
On restera	On partira	On répondra
Nous resterons	Nous partirons	Nous répondrons
Vous resterez	Vous partirez	Vous répondrez
Ils resteront	Ils partiront	Ils répondront
Elles resteront	Elles partiront	Elles répondront

NB The future tense is often used with expressions like **quand, lorsque, au moment où, dès que, aussitôt que**. Ex.: **Quand** vous **arriverez**, nous **serons** rassurés.

Irregular Future Stems

aller	→ j'irai		recevoir	→ je recevrai
avoir	→ j'aurai		savoir	→ je saurai
apercevoir *to see*	→ j'apercevrai		tenir	→ je tiendrai
courir	→ je courrai		voir	→ je verrai
cueillir *to pick, to gather*	→ je cueillerai		vouloir	→ je voudrai
devoir	→ je devrai		venir	→ je viendrai
être	→ je serai		valoir	→ je vaudrai
envoyer	→ j'enverrai			
faire	→ je ferai		*(to be worth)*	
falloir *have to*	→ il faudra			
mourir	→ je mourrai		**Other Irregular Verbs:**	
pleuvoir *to rain*	→ il pleuvra		appeler	→ j'appellerai
pouvoir	→ je pourrai		jeter	→ je jetterai
			acheter	→ j'achèterai
			nettoyer	→ je nettoierai

1
h

1i Recent Past, Present Progressive: Passé récent, Présent progressif

Recent Past: Passé récent

Definition: The RECENT PAST expresses what a person HAS JUST DONE. In order to form the RECENT PAST, conjugate the verb VENIR in the present tense, then add DE/D' and then the INFINITIVE:

$$\text{VENIR} + \text{DE/D'} + \text{INFINITIVE}$$

Example: Dominique **vient de facturer** le client.
(Dominique has just invoiced the client.)

SUBJECT	VENIR IN THE PRESENT TENSE	DE/D'	INFINITIVE
Je	viens	de	commencer
Tu	viens	d'	arriver
Il	vient	de	répondre
Elle	vient	de	sortir
On	vient	d'	essayer
Nous	venons	de	comprendre
Vous	venez	de	résumer
Ils	viennent	de	s'endormir
Elles	viennent	d'	inviter

NB | Never use the passé composé with the recent past. Always use the imparfait.
Ex.: Vous **veniez** de faire le ménage. (You had just done the housework.)
Fabienne **venait** de s'habiller. (Fabienne had just got dressed.)

Present Progressive: Présent progressif

Definition: The PRESENT PROGRESSIVE expresses what a person IS DOING/ IS BUSY DOING or IS IN THE PROCESS OF DOING. In order to form the PRESENT PROGRESSIVE, conjugate the verb ÊTRE in the present tense, then add EN TRAIN DE/D' and then add the INFINITIVE:

ÊTRE + EN TRAIN DE/D' + INFINITIVE

Example: Je **suis en train de faire** mes valises.
(I am in the process of packing my suitcase.)

SUBJECT	ÊTRE EN TRAIN DE/D'	INFINITIVE
Je	suis en train de	travailler
Tu	es en train de	pleurer
Il	est en train de	mentir
Elle	est en train de	dormir
On	est en train de	discuter
Nous	sommes en train de	gagner
Vous	êtes en train de	perdre
Ils	sont en train d'	apprendre
Elles	sont en train de	déjeuner

NB The present progressive can also be used with other tenses.
Ex.: J'**étais** en train de conduire. (I was busy driving.)
Il **sera** en train de travailler. (He will be busy working.)

1j   Present Perfect: Passé composé

Definition: The PASSÉ COMPOSÉ is used to describe a single completed action in the past. In order to form the PASSÉ COMPOSÉ, take the auxiliary verb AVOIR, conjugate it in the PRESENT TENSE and add the PAST PARTICIPLE.

Example: Il a oublié. (He forgot.)

VERB ENDING	INFINITIVE	PAST PARTICIPLE	EXAMPLE
ER	PARLER	PARLÉ	J'ai parlé (I spoke / I have spoken)
IR	FINIR	FINI	J'ai fini (I finished / I have finished)
RE	VENDRE	VENDU	J'ai vendu (I sold / I have sold)

Parler	Finir	Vendre
J'ai parlé	J'ai fini	J'ai vendu
Tu as parlé	Tu as fini	Tu as vendu
Il a parlé	Il a fini	Il a vendu
Elle a parlé	Elle a fini	Elle a vendu
On a parlé	On a fini	On a vendu
Nous **avons** parlé	Nous **avons** fini	Nous **avons** vendu
Vous **avez** parlé	Vous **avez** fini	Vous **avez** vendu
Ils **ont** parlé	Ils **ont** fini	Ils **ont** vendu
Elles **ont** parlé	Elles **ont** fini	Elles **ont** vendu

NB | The past participle for all ER verbs always ends in É (garder–gardé). Irregular past participles are either IR or RE verbs.

Irregular Past Participles

avoir	→ eu	mourir	→ mort
apercevoir	→ aperçu	naître	→ né
apprendre	→ appris	offrir	→ offert
atteindre	→ atteint	ouvrir	→ ouvert
boire	→ bu	plaindre *to complain*	→ plaint
couvrir	→ couvert	pleuvoir	→ plu
craindre	→ craint	produire	→ produit
convenir *to suit*	→ convenu	peindre	→ peint
courir *to suit*	→ couru	paraître *to appear*	→ paru
concevoir *to conceive*	→ conçu	prendre	→ pris
connaître	→ connu	plaire	→ plu
conduire	→ conduit	pouvoir	→ pu
comprendre	→ compris	rire	→ ri
construire	→ construit	reprendre	→ repris
croire	→ cru	revenir	→ revenu
dire	→ dit	reconnaître	→ reconnu
devoir	→ dû	recevoir	→ reçu
décevoir	→ déçu	suffire	→ suffi
devenir	→ devenu	suivre	→ suivi
disparaître	→ disparu	savoir	→ su
déplaire *displease*	→ déplu	secourir *to help, to aid*	→ secouru
découvrir	→ découvert	survivre	→ survécu
décrire	→ décrit	sourire	→ souri
détruire	→ détruit	surprendre *surprise*	→ surpris
écrire	→ écrit	souffrir	→ souffert
éteindre *turn off, unwind of, extinguish*	→ éteint	traduire	→ traduit
élire *to elect*	→ élu	tenir	→ tenu
être	→ été	taire *to hush up*	→ tu
faire	→ fait	venir	→ venu
falloir	→ fallu	vouloir	→ voulu
joindre	→ joint	voir	→ vu
lire	→ lu	valoir	→ valu
mettre	→ mis	vivre	→ vécu

1k To Be or Not to Be in the Present Perfect: Être au passé composé

Definition: 99% of all verbs take the auxiliary verb AVOIR in the PASSÉ COMPOSÉ. However, the following verbs take ÊTRE in the PASSÉ COMPOSÉ. They are usually verbs indicating a movement such as to go, to come, to arrive, to leave, to return. In order to remember the verbs that take ÊTRE, use the mnemonic **DR MRS VANDERTRAMPP**:

INFINITIVE	PAST PARTICIPLE	ENGLISH TRANSLATION
descendre	descendu	to go down/to get out of (a car)
revenir	revenu	to come back
mourir	mort	to die
rentrer	rentré	to return
sortir	sorti	to go out
venir	venu	to come
arriver	arrivé	to arrive
naître	né	to be born
devenir	devenu	to become
entrer	entré	to enter
rester	resté	to stay
tomber	tombé	to fall
retourner	retourné	to return
aller	allé	to go
monter	monté	to go up/to get into (a car)
partir	parti	to leave
passer	passé	to pass by
+ All reflexive verbs: se coucher, s'endormir, s'habiller, se reposer, etc.		

NB | Use **avoir** when PASSER means TO SPEND/TO PASS. Use être when it means TO PASS BY.
The verb DÉCÉDER (to die), also takes être. Ex.: Il **est** décédé le 18 février 2005.

With **ÊTRE** verbs, the past participle agrees in gender and number with the subject:

RENTRER	VENIR
Je **suis** rentré(e)	Je **suis** venu(e)
Tu **es** rentré(e)	Tu **es** venu(e)
Il **est** rentré_	Il **est** venu_
Elle **est** rentrée	Elle **est** venue
On **est** rentré(s)(es)	On **est** venu(s)(es)
Nous **sommes** rentrés(es)	Nous **sommes** venus(es)
Vous **êtes** rentré(e)(s)(es)	Vous **êtes** venu(e)(s)(es)
Ils **sont** rentrés	Ils **sont** venus
Elles **sont** rentrées	Elles **sont** venues

NB | When **ON** means WE, the past participle agrees with the subject.
Ex.: **On s'est vus** hier soir. (masculine plural)
On s'est croisées jeudi après le cours. (feminine plural)

All reflexive verbs take ÊTRE in the passé composé:

Se réveiller
Je me **suis** réveillé(e)
Tu t'**es** réveillé(e)
Il s'**est** reveillé_ / Elle s'**est** réveillée / On s'**est** réveillé(s)(es)
Nous nous **sommes** réveillés(es)
Vous vous **êtes** réveillé(e)(s)(es)
Ils se **sont** réveillés / Elles se **sont** réveillées

NB | When the verbs **monter, descendre, rentrer** and **sortir** are followed by a direct object then use **avoir** and not **être**. Ex.: J'**ai** monté l'escalier. Elle **a** descendu la piste. Vous **avez** rentré vos affaires.

she went the down track

1I Imperfect: Imparfait

Definition: The IMPERFECT is used to indicate a continuous or repeated action in the past. It is also used for descriptions in the past and states of mind or emotion.

IMPARFAIT	PASSÉ COMPOSÉ
Elle dînait quand ...	son mari a appelé
She was eating dinner when . . .	her husband called

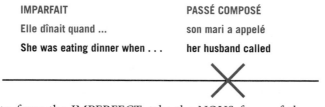

In order to form the IMPERFECT, take the NOUS form of the verb in the PRESENT TENSE, drop the ONS and add **AIS, AIS, AIT, IONS, IEZ, AIENT**:

> **Rester → Nous rest[ons]**
> Je restais
> Tu restais
> Il restait
> Elle restait
> On restait
> Nous restions
> Vous restiez
> Ils restaient
> Elles restaient

Some Irregular Verbs in the Imperfect

être   → j'étais, tu étais, il était, nous étions, vous étiez, ils étaient

NB | The nous form of **être** is "nous **sommes**." Thus the root of the imparfait is derived from the infinitive **être** → **ét_**.

manger   → je mangeais, tu mangeais, il mangeait, nous mangions, vous mangiez, ils mangeaient

commencer   → je commençais, tu commençais, il commençait, nous commencions, vous commenciez, ils commençaient

When to Use the Imparfait

1. **Was/were doing:**

   Elle chantait.   (She was singing.)

   Je travaillais.   (I was working.)

2. **Used to do:**

   Vous jouiez aux échecs.   (You used to play chess.)

   Tu pleurais beaucoup.   (You used to cry a lot.)

3. **Repeated action in the past:**

   The imperfect is used with expressions that indicate an action that is repeated in the past, such as **toujours, fréquemment, d'habitude, souvent, quelquefois, parfois, de temps en temps, tous les jours, chaque jour/mois/semaine, le lundi/le mardi,** etc.

   Ex.: Tous les étés, j'allais à la plage. (Every summer I went to the beach.)

4. **A state of mind or an emotion:**

   Il réfléchissait. Elle était heureuse. On désirait partir.

5. **Describing the past:**

   Il faisait beau, il portait une chemise blanche et les étoiles brillaient dans le ciel.

6. **The imparfait is frequently used with the following verbs:**

   aimer/avoir/être/croire/désirer/espérer/penser/pouvoir/vouloir/ savoir/regretter

7. **With the expression si when you are making a suggestion:**

   Ex.: **Si** on allait au cinéma!

   (How about going to the movies!)

1
I

1m Present Participle, Gerund: Participe présent, Gérondif

Present Participle: Participe présent

Definition: The PRESENT PARTICIPLE of TO WAIT is WAITING. In order to form the PRESENT PARTICIPLE, take the **NOUS** form of the PRESENT TENSE, drop the **ONS** and add **ANT**:

INFINITIVE	NOUS FORM OF PRESENT	PRESENT PARTICIPLE
parler	nous parl**ons**	parl**ant** (speaking)
finir	nous finiss**ons**	finiss**ant** (finishing)
répondre	nous répond**ons**	répond**ant** (answering)
dire	nous dis**ons**	dis**ant** (saying)

Irregular Present Participles

INFINITIVE	NOUS FORM OF PRESENT	IRREGULAR PRESENT PARTICIPLE
avoir	nous avons	ayant (having)
être	nous sommes	étant (being)
savoir	nous savons	sachant (knowing)

> **NB** Combining the present participle of AVOIR and ÊTRE with the past participle: **ayant** commencé (having begun), **ayant** vu (having seen), **étant** arrivé (having arrived).

The present participle can sometimes be used as a noun:

un particip**ant**	un pass**ant**	un gagn**ant**
un début**ant**	un commerç**ant**	un fabric**ant**

The present participle can sometimes be used as an adjective:

un jeune homme charm**ant**	→ une jeune femme charm**ante**
un roman passionn**ant**	→ une nouvelle passionn**ante**
des films intéress**ants**	→ des pièces intéress**antes**

> **NB** If the present participle is used either as a noun or an adjective, it must often be adjusted in terms of gender and number: **un** dirigeant → **une** dirigeante, **un** passant → **une** passante, **un** commerçant → **une** commerçante, l'eau rafraîchissante.

Gerund: Gérondif

Definition: The GERUND of TO WAIT is WHILE WAITING:

INFINITIVE	PRESENT PARTICIPLE	GERUND
parler	parl**ant** (speaking)	en parl**ant** (while speaking)
finir	finiss**ant** (finishing)	en finiss**ant** (while finishing)
répondre	répond**ant** (answering)	en répond**ant** (while answering)
dormir	dorm**ant** (sleeping)	en dorm**ant** (while sleeping)
avoir	ay**ant** (having)	en ay**ant** (while having)
être	ét**ant** (being)	en ét**ant** (while being)
savoir	sach**ant** (knowing)	en sach**ant** (while knowing)

1
m

Ex.: On apprend le français **en** étudi**ant**!
     (One learns French while studying!)

1n Imperative: Impératif

Definition: The IMPERATIVE is the equivalent of giving someone a COMMAND, a REQUEST, a SUGGESTION or an ORDER. It only exists in the TU, **NOUS** and VOUS forms. In order to form the IMPERATIVE, simply take the tu, nous and vous forms of the PRESENT TENSE:

Arrête! (Stop!)	=	command given to **tu**
Arrêtons! (Let's stop!)	=	command given to **nous**
Arrêtez! (Stop!)	=	command given to **vous**

Parler	Finir	Attendre
Parle!	Finis!	Attends!
Parlons!	Finissons!	Attendons!
Parlez!	Finissez!	Attendez!

NB | With **ER** verbs, drop the S in the TU form, but retain it with IR and RE verbs:

Parler	→ Parle_!		Demander	→ Demande_!
Finir	→ Finis!		Choisir	→ Choisis!
Vendre	→ Vends!		Répondre	→ Réponds!

Irregular Imperatives

Être	Avoir	Savoir
Sois!	Aie!	Sache!
Soyons!	Ayons!	Sachons!
Soyez!	Ayez!	Sachez!

NB | **Veuillez** is the formal imperative of "vouloir." It is translated as "Kindly . . . "

A Few Slightly Irregular Imperatives

Offrir	Nettoyer	Appeler	Manger	Acheter
Offre!	Nettoie!	Appelle!	Mange!	Achète!
Offrons!	Nettoyons!	Appelons!	Mangeons!	Achetons!
Offrez!	Nettoyez!	Appelez!	Mangez!	Achetez!

The Imperative with Reflexive Verbs

Se réveiller

Réveille-toi!	but	Ne te réveille **pas!**
Réveillons-nous!	but	Ne nous réveillons **pas!**
Réveillez-vous!	but	Ne vous réveillez **pas!**

NB When the imperative is in the affirmative, the direct or indirect object pronoun follows the verb (here, ME changes to **MOI** and TE changes to **TOI**).

Rends-**le-moi!**	but	Ne me le rends **pas!**
Parlez-**lui-en!**	but	Ne lui en parlez **pas!**
Dépêche-**toi!**	but	Ne te dépêche **pas!**
Allez-**vous-en!**	but	Ne vous en allez **pas!**

The imperative does not exist in the THIRD PERSON. If needed, you can use it with the PRESENT SUBJUNCTIVE:

Qu'il finisse tout de suite!   (He should finish immediately.)
Qu'elles fassent attention!   (They should pay attention.)

1o Conditional: Conditionnel

Definition: The CONDITIONAL is used to indicate what one would do. In order to form the conditional, start by taking the INFINITIVE form of the verb, just as you did with the FUTURE. Then add the IMPERFECT ENDINGS AIS, AIS, AIT, IONS, IEZ, AIENT. With RE verbs, the E falls away:

Example: Je parlerais. (I would speak.)

Rester	Partir	Répondre
Je resterais	Je partirais	Je répondrais
Tu resterais	Tu partirais	Tu répondrais
Il resterait	Il partirait	Il répondrait
Elle resterait	Elle partirait	Elle répondrait
On resterait	On partirait	On répondrait
Nous resterions	Nous partirions	Nous répondrions
Vous resteriez	Vous partiriez	Vous répondriez
Ils resteraient	Ils partiraient	Ils répondraient
Elles resteraient	Elles partiraient	Elles répondraient

Irregular Conditional Stems = Irregular Future Stems

aller	→ j'irais	mourir	→ je mourrais
avoir	→ j'aurais	pleuvoir	→ il pleuvrait
apercevoir	→ j'apercevrais	pouvoir	→ je pourrais
courir	→ je courrais	recevoir	→ je recevrais
cueillir	→ je cueillerais	savoir	→ je saurais
devoir	→ je devrais	tenir	→ je tiendrais
être	→ je serais	voir	→ je verrais
envoyer	→ j'enverrais	vouloir	→ je voudrais
faire	→ je ferais	venir	→ je viendrais
falloir	→ il faudrait	valoir	→ je vaudrais

Other Irregular Verbs in the Conditional

appeler	→ j'appellerais
jeter	→ je jetterais
acheter	→ j'achèterais
nettoyer	→ je nettoierais

NB | The verbs **pouvoir, vouloir** and **aimer** are often used in the conditional when you want to be polite. This is called le **conditionnel de politesse**.

Je **voudrais** un café.

Tu **voudrais** prendre un verre?

Vous **pourriez** compter sur moi.

Voudriez-vous dîner avec moi?

Aimeriez-vous venir à midi?

Je **pourrais** vous aider?

The IF or SI clause

Never put **RAI** (future or conditional) in the **SI** clause!

SI CLAUSE	SECONDARY CLAUSE	EXAMPLE
Si + présent	futur/impératif/présent	Si vous **venez** à l'hôtel, **j'attendrai**.
Si + imparfait	conditionnel	Si vous **aviez** le temps, je **viendrais**.
Si + plus-que-parfait	conditionnel passé	Si vous **étiez partie**, **j'aurais pleuré**.

1p Subjunctive: Subjonctif

Definition: The SUBJUNCTIVE is a MOOD that is found in the SECOND or SUBORDINATE CLAUSE of a sentence. It usually comes after the word QUE and must correspond with the NECESSITY, EMOTION, DOUBT, WISH or CONDITION expressed in the MAIN or PRINCIPAL CLAUSE of the sentence.

MAIN CLAUSE EXPRESSING EMOTION	QUE	SUBJUNCTIVE CLAUSE
Elle est heureuse	QUE	sa nièce soit douée.

In order to form the SUBJUNCTIVE, take the ILS/ELLES form of the PRESENT TENSE, drop the ENT and add E, ES, E, IONS, IEZ, ENT:

PENSER (ils pensent)	REMPLIR (ils remplissent)	RENDRE (ils rendent)
que je pense	que je remplisse	que je rende
que tu penses	que tu remplisses	que tu rendes
qu'il pense	qu'il remplisse	qu'il rende
qu'elle pense	qu'elle remplisse	qu'elle rende
qu'on pense	qu'on remplisse	qu'on rende
que nous pensions	que nous remplissions	que nous rendions
que vous pensiez	que vous remplissiez	que vous rendiez
qu'ils pensent	qu'ils remplissent	qu'ils rendent
qu'elles pensent	qu'elles remplissent	qu'elles rendent

Irregular Subjunctive Verbs

être	→ que je sois, tu sois, il soit, nous soyons, vous soyez, ils soient
avoir	→ que j'aie, tu aies, il ait, nous ayons, vous ayez, ils aient
aller	→ que j'aille, tu ailles, il aille, nous allions, vous alliez, ils aillent
faire	→ que je fasse, tu fasses, il fasse, nous fassions, vous fassiez, ils fassent
pouvoir	→ que je puisse, tu puisses, il puisse, nous puissions, vous puissiez, ils puissent
vouloir	→ que je veuille, tu veuilles, il veuille, nous voulions, vous vouliez, ils veuillent

continued

continued

savoir	→ que je **sache**, tu **saches**, il **sache**, nous **sachions**, vous **sachiez**, ils **sachent**
falloir	→ qu'il **faille**
pleuvoir	→ qu'il **pleuve**

When to Use the Subjunctive

1. **Wishing/wanting/desiring:**
   Je **veux** que tu **viennes**.

2. **Doubt:**
   Elle **doute** qu'il **soit** à l'heure.

3. **Feelings/emotions:**
   Vous êtes **content** que je **comprenne**.

4. **Ordering/commanding:**
   Il **exige** que nous **fassions** le travail.

5. **Necessity:**
   Il est **nécessaire** que vous **jouiez** le match.

6. **With the comparative:**
   Elle est plus charmante que vous ne **croyiez**.

7. **With the following expressions:**
   il faut que, il vaut mieux que, il est essentiel que, il est possible que, il est impossible que, il est peu probable que, il est important que, il est préférable que, il est douteux que, c'est dommage que, il est regrettable que, il semble que, il est surprenant que, avant que, jusqu'à ce que, sans que, afin que, pour que, de manière que, de sorte que, de peur que, bien que, quoique, à condition que, pourvu que, à moins que.

   And with the following negative clauses:
   il n'est pas probable que, il n'est pas vrai que, il ne me semble pas que, il ne paraît pas que, je ne crois pas que, je ne pense pas que.

8. **As an imperative in the 3rd person:**
   Vive la reine! Ainsi soit-il!

NB | DON'T use the subjunctive with the following expressions: **il est probable que, il est vrai que, il me semble que, il paraît que, aussitôt que, dès que, après que, pendant que, parce que, croire que, espérer que, penser que!**

1q Past Historic: Passé simple

Definition: The PAST HISTORIC (PASSÉ SIMPLE) is the equivalent of the PRESENT PERFECT (PASSÉ COMPOSÉ) but is used almost exclusively as a LITERARY TENSE. It is NOT COMMON in everyday CONVERSATIONAL and WRITTEN French.

Example: Il parla. (He spoke.) PASSÉ SIMPLE
Il a parlé. (He spoke.) PASSÉ COMPOSÉ

Forming the Past Historic

For **ER** verbs, drop the **ER** and add **AI, AS, A, ÂMES, ÂTES, ÈRENT**:

TROUVER	ALLER
Je trouvai	J'allai
Tu trouvas	Tu allas
Il trouva	Il alla
Elle trouva	Elle alla
On trouva	On alla
Nous trouvâmes	Nous allâmes
Vous trouvâtes	Vous allâtes
Ils trouvèrent	Ils allèrent
Elles trouvèrent	Elles allèrent

For **IR** and **RE** verbs, drop the **IR/RE** and add **IS, IS, IT, ÎMES, ÎTES, IRENT**:

CHOISIR	ATTENDRE
Je choisis	J'attendis
Tu choisis	Tu attendis
Il choisit	Il attendit
Elle choisit	Elle attendit
On choisit	On attendit
Nous choisîmes	Nous attendîmes
Vous choisîtes	Vous attendîtes
Ils choisirent	Ils attendirent
Elles choisirent	Elles attendirent

Irregular Verbs in the Past Historic

Take the ROOT from the PAST PARTICIPLE:

pouvoir	→ je pus, tu pus, il put, nous pûmes, vous pûtes, ils purent
avoir	→ j'eus, tu eus, il eut, nous eûmes, vous eûtes, ils eurent
croire	→ je crus, tu crus, il crut, nous crûmes, vous crûtes, ils crurent
mettre	→ je mis, tu mis, il mit, nous mîmes, vous mîtes, ils mirent
prendre	→ je pris, tu pris, il prit, nous prîmes, vous prîtes, ils prirent
savoir	→ je sus, tu sus, il sut, nous sûmes, vous sûtes, ils surent
boire	→ je bus, tu bus, il but, nous bûmes, vous bûtes, ils burent
lire	→ je lus, tu lus, il lut, nous lûmes, vous lûtes, ils lurent
vouloir	→ je voulus, tu voulus, il voulut, nous voulûmes, vous voulûtes, ils voulurent
connaître	→ je connus, tu connus, il connut, nous connûmes, vous connûtes, ils connurent

BUT:

ÊTRE	→ je fus, tu fus, il fut, nous fûmes, vous fûtes, ils furent
VOIR	→ je vis, tu vis, il vit, nous vîmes, vous vîtes, ils virent
VENIR	→ je vins, tu vins, il vint, nous vînmes, vous vîntes, ils vinrent
ÉCRIRE	→ j'écrivis, tu écrivis, il écrivit, nous écrivîmes, vous écrivîtes, ils écrivirent

1r That Tricky Past Participle: Le participe passé à la portée de tous

1. When the verb is conjugated with the auxiliary verb ÊTRE, then the past participle agrees with the subject of the verb.

NORMAL ÊTRE VERB
Je suis parti(**e**)
Tu es allé(**e**)
Il est monté_
Elle est sortie
On est entré(**s**)(**es**)
Nous sommes devenus(**es**)
Vous êtes tombé(**e**)(**s**)(**es**)
Ils sont restés
Elles sont arriv**ées**

2. With reflexive verbs, the past participle agrees with the reflexive pronoun only if the verb itself takes a direct object.

A REFLEXIVE VERB THAT TAKES A DIRECT OBJECT	
Je **me** suis réveillé(**e**)	→ réveiller **quelqu'un**
Tu **t'**es couché(**e**)	→ coucher **quelqu'un**
Il **s'**est habillé_	→ habiller **quelqu'un**
Elle **s'**est maquill**ée**	→ maquiller **quelqu'un**
On **s'**est rencontré(**s**)(**es**)	→ rencontrer **quelqu'un**
Nous **nous** sommes levés(**es**)	→ lever **quelqu'un**
Vous **vous** êtes lavé(**e**)(**s**)(**es**)	→ laver **quelqu'un**
Ils **se** sont vu**s**	→ voir **quelqu'un**
Elles **se** sont amus**ées**	→ amuser **quelqu'un**

NB | Here the reflexive pronoun **me/te/se/nous/vous/se** is the direct object!

3. **When the reflexive verb takes an indirect object there is no agreement:**

je me suis dit	dire à **quelqu'un**
tu t'es lavé les mains	laver les mains à **quelqu'un**
	(les mains = direct object)
elle s'est maquillé le visage	maquiller le visage à **quelqu'un**
	(le visage = direct object)
nous nous sommes demandé	demander à **quelqu'un**
vous vous êtes parlé	parler à **quelqu'un**
ils se sont téléphoné	téléphoner à **quelqu'un**
elles se sont écrit	écrire à **quelqu'un**

NB | Here the reflexive part of the verb **me/te/se/nous/vous/se** is the indirect object!

4. **When the verb is preceded by a direct object, the past participle must agree with the gender and number of the direct object:**

J'ai vu **la belle maison.**	Je l'ai vu**e.**
Vous avez lu **les revues.**	Vous **les** avez lu**es.**
Tu as rencontré **ma copine.**	Tu l'as rencontré**e.**
Elle s'est lavé **les cheveux.**	Elle se **les** est lavé**s.**
Il a offert **les fleurs** à Simone.	**Les fleurs** qu'il a offert**es** à Simone sont belles.
Ils ont lu **les journaux.**	**Les journaux** qu'ils ont lu**s** sont intéressants.

NB | Past participles are invariable for: **s'imaginer, se rendre compte, se plaire**.

NB | If the past participle is followed by an infinitive or by a direct object, then the past participle does not agree:

Elle s'est **fait couper** les cheveux.	Ils se sont **fait réviser** leurs voitures.
Elles se sont **acheté les robes.**	Nous nous sommes **donné rendez-vous.**

NB | Sometimes the adjective looks exactly like the past participle. Ex.: la solution proposé**e**, les mains levé**es**, les femmes aimé**es**, les distributeurs agréé**s**

5. **In the passive voice the past participle must also agree:**

La couturière a fait cette robe.	**Cette robe** a été fai**te** par la couturière.
La femme a acheté les jupes.	**Les jupes** ont été achet**ées** par la femme.
L'étudiant écrira la composition.	**La composition** sera écri**te** par l'étudiant.
Les ouvriers prennent une pause.	**Une pause** est pri**se** par les ouvriers.
Le pâtissier prépare les gâteaux.	**Les gâteaux** sont prépar**és** par le pâtissier.

1s Compound Tenses: Temps composés

When we formed the PRESENT PERFECT (PASSÉ COMPOSÉ), we used the construction: PRONOUN + AVOIR/ÊTRE in the PRESENT TENSE + PAST PARTICIPLE. Ex.: **elle a constaté / vous avez remarqué**.

The very SAME PRINCIPLE applies to all the other COMPOUND TENSES! All you have to do to create the COMPOUND TENSE of a given tense is to decide whether it is an AVOIR or an ÊTRE verb (see pages 21 and 22). Once you have worked this out, put AVOIR or ÊTRE in the very tense that you're dealing with and simply add the PAST PARTICIPLE!

Pluperfect: Plus-que-parfait

Let's take the imperfect for example. We're going to form the pluperfect tense (past of the imperfect), which is called the plus-que-parfait:

FERMER (imparfait)	FERMER (plus-que-parfait) (takes AVOIR)
Je fermais (I was closing)	J'**avais** fermé (I had closed)
Tu fermais	Tu **avais** fermé
Il fermait	Il **avait** fermé
Nous fermions	Nous **avions** fermé
Vous fermiez	Vous **aviez** fermé
Ils fermaient	Ils **avaient** fermé

SORTIR (imparfait)	SORTIR (plus-que-parfait) (takes ÊTRE)
Je sortais (I was going out)	J'**étais** sorti(**e**) (I had gone out)
Tu sortais	Tu **étais** sorti(**e**)
Il sortait	Il **était** sorti_ / Elle **était** sortie
Nous sortions	Nous **étions** sortis(**es**)
Vous sortiez	Vous **étiez** sorti(**e**)(**s**)(**es**)
Ils sortaient	Ils **étaient** sortis / Elles **étaient** sorties

Conditional Perfect: Conditionnel passé

Let's take the conditional tense and form the conditional perfect tense (past of the conditional), which is called the conditionnel passé:

TROUVER (conditional)	TROUVER (conditionnel passé) (takes AVOIR)
Je trouverais (I would find)	J'**aurais** trouvé (I would have found)
Tu trouverais	Tu **aurais** trouvé
Il trouverait	Il **aurait** trouvé
Nous trouverions	Nous **aurions** trouvé
Vous trouveriez	Vous **auriez** trouvé
Ils trouveraient	Ils **auraient** trouvé

Future Perfect: Futur antérieur

Let's take the simple futur tense and form the future perfect (past of the future), which is called the futur antérieur:

PARTIR (futur)	PARTIR (futur antérieur) (takes ÊTRE)
Je partirai (I will leave)	Je **serai** parti(**e**) (I will have left)
Tu partiras	Tu **seras** parti(**e**)
Il partira	Il **sera** parti_ / Elle **sera** partie
Nous partirons	Nous **serons** partis(**es**)
Vous partirez	Vous **serez** parti(**e**)(**s**)(**es**)
Ils partiront	Ils **seront** partis / Elles **seront** parties

NB | In the same way, you can form the past of the subjunctive. Ex.: Il fallait que vous **soyez** parti à l'heure. Or the past of the past historic. Ex.: Il **fut** venu, nous **eûmes** discuté, elle **eut** chanté.

1t Interrogative: Interrogation

Definition: The INTERROGATIVE is used to ask a question.

There are four possible structures to a question:
1. Vous parlez anglais?
2. **Est-ce que** vous parlez anglais?
3. **Parlez-vous** anglais? (inversion of "vous parlez" → **parlez-vous**)
4. Vous parlez anglais, **n'est-ce pas?** (Seeking confirmation or denial)

What happens in a compound tense?
1. Vous avez compris?
2. **Est-ce que** vous avez compris?
3. **Avez-vous** compris?

When EST-CE QUE is followed by a vowel, the QUE becomes QU':
Ex.: Est-ce **qu'il** vient demain?

   Est-ce **qu'elles** seront présentes?

When inverting the verb and the pronoun, add the hyphen:
Ex.: Parlez-vous français?

AVOIR	INVERSION OF THE SUBJECT AND THE VERB	
J'ai	**ai-je?**	(**puis-je** and **suis-je** are also exceptionally used in the JE form)
Tu as	**as-tu?**	
Il a	**a-t-il?**	(add the "t" between the two consecutive vowels)
Elle a	**a-t-elle?**	(add the "t" between the two consecutive vowels)
On a	**a-t-on?**	(add the "t" between the two consecutive vowels)
Nous avons	**avons-nous?**	
Vous avez	**avez-vous?**	
Ils ont	**ont-ils?**	
Elles ont	**ont-elles?**	

PARLER	PRÉSENT	PASSÉ COMPOSÉ	FUTUR
Je parle	est-ce que je parle?	**ai-je** parlé?	**parlerai-je?**
Tu parles	**parles-tu?**	**as-tu** parlé?	**parleras-tu?**
Il parle	**parle-t-il?**	**a-t-il** parlé?	**parlera-t-il?**
Elle parle	**parle-t-elle?**	**a-t-elle** parlé?	**parlera-t-elle?**
On parle	**parle-t-on?**	**a-t-on** parlé?	**parlera-t-on?**
Nous parlons	**parlons-nous?**	**avons-nous** parlé?	**parlerons-nous?**
Vous parlez	**parlez-vous?**	**avez-vous** parlé?	**parlerez-vous?**
Ils parlent	**parlent-ils?**	**ont-ils** parlé?	**parleront-ils?**
Elles parlent	**parlent-elles?**	**ont-elles** parlé?	**parleront-elles?**

Common Question Words:

combien = how much   **comment** = how   **où** = where
pourquoi = why   **quand** = when   **qui** = who
quoi = what   **quel/quelle/quels/quelles** = which/what

If the question word starts the sentence, then make the inversion:

Où **avez-vous** appris le français?   Quand **viendras-tu?**
Combien de personnes y **a-t-il** dans la salle?   Comment **allez-vous?**

BUT:

Don't make the inversion if the expression **est-ce que** precedes the noun/pronoun:
Ex.: Où **est-ce que vous avez appris** le français? Quand **est-ce que** Patrick est rentré?

NB | The inversion is also made after the quotation marks in direct speech.
Ex.: « Je crois que le résultat parle de lui-même », **a-t-il** affirmé.

1
t

1u Negative: Négation

Definition: The NEGATIVE expresses a NEGATION, REFUSAL OR DENIAL.
In French, the NEGATIVE is usually made up of **NE** and **PAS** which are generally
positioned on either side of the conjugated verb:

AFFIRMATIVE	NEGATIVE
Il parle italien.	Il **ne** parle **pas** italien.
Elle écrit la lettre.	Elle **n'**écrit **pas** la lettre.
Elle se maquillera.	Elle **ne** se maquillera **pas**.
Je vais me coucher.	Je **ne** vais **pas** me coucher.
Elle a dérangé les invités.	Elle **n'a pas** dérangé les invités.
Vous vous êtes habillée.	Vous **ne** vous êtes **pas** habillée.

Il donne.	Il **ne** donne **pas**.
Il me donne.	Il **ne** me donne **pas**.
Il me le donne.	Il **ne** me le donne **pas**.
Il me l'a donné.	Il **ne** me l'a **pas** donné.

BUT: Il m'a dit de **ne pas** téléphoner, de **ne pas** commencer et de **ne pas** bouger.

NB In the negative **du, de la, de l'** and **des** all change to **DE** or **D'**:
Est-ce que vous avez **des** problèmes?   Non, je n'ai pas **de** problèmes.
Est-ce que vous voulez **de l'**eau ?   Non, je ne veux pas **d'**eau.

Different Negative Constructions

Negative Expression	English Translation	Example
ne... pas encore	not yet	Il n'a pas encore son diplôme.
ne... pas du tout	not at all	Il ne cuisine pas du tout.
ne... point	not (emphatic)	Il ne le dit point.
ne... plus	no longer/no more	Il ne fume plus.
ne... jamais	never	Il ne ment jamais.
ne... guère	hardly	Il ne va guère en vacances.
ne... aucun(e)	not any	Il n'a aucun livre.
aucun(e)... ne	none	Aucun film n'est intéressant.
ne... rien	nothing/anything	Il ne voit rien.
rien... ne	nothing (subject)	Rien ne peut m'aider.
ne... personne	no one/anyone	Il ne regarde personne.
personne... ne	no one (subject)	Personne n'est venu.
nul... ne	no one (subject)	Nul ne sait la vérité.
ne... ni... ni	neither nor	Il n'a ni sœur ni frère.
ne... non plus	neither/either	Je ne le sais pas non plus.

NB | Sometimes NE and PAS don't sandwich the conjugated verb. Ex.: **Personne n'**est venu. **Rien ne** peut m'aider. Il n'a **ni** sœur **ni** frère.

NB | Remember that the combination NE... QUE means ONLY! Ex.: Elle **ne** lit **que** les revues et son mari **ne** lit **que** les journaux.

Negative of the Imperative

Travaille!	Ne travaille pas!
Écoutez!	N'écoutez pas!
Réveille-toi!	Ne te réveille pas!
Dépêchez-vous!	Ne vous dépêchez pas!
Prends-le!	Ne le prends pas!
Allez-y!	N'y allez pas!
Envoyez-le-moi!	Ne me l'envoyez pas!
Dis-le-lui!	Ne le lui dis pas!

NB | When you want to contradict someone who asks you a question in the negative, use **SI** and not **OUI**. Ex.: Vous n'avez pas pris l'argent? **Si**, je l'ai pris.

1v Comparative, Superlative: Comparatif, Superlatif

Comparative: Comparatif

Definition: The COMPARATIVE is used when expressing a degree of comparison between people or things.

plus... que

Fabien est **plus** intelligent_ **que** Delphine.
(Fabien is more intelligent than Delphine.)
Delphine est **plus** intelligent**e que** Fabien.
(The ADJECTIVE agrees with the SUBJECT)
Delphine et Françoise sont plus intelligent**es** que Fabien et Luc.

aussi... que

Fabien est **aussi** intelligent_ **que** Delphine.
(Fabien is as intelligent as Delphine.)
Delphine est **aussi** intelligent**e que** Fabien.

moins... que

Fabien est **moins** intelligent_ **que** Delphine.
(Fabien is less intelligent than Delphine.)
Delphine est **moins** intelligent**e que** Fabien.
Fabien et Luc sont moins intelligent**s** que Delphine et Françoise.

The comparative followed by a noun or a number takes DE:

Elle a **plus de** copines que sa sœur.
Il a **moins de** chance que son frère.
Bastien travaille **moins de** trente-cinq heures par semaine.
Camille parle **plus de** quatre langues étrangères.

Adverbs don't have gender, so in the comparative they remain unchanged:

Vous répondez plus/moins/aussi **calmement** que lui.
Elle court plus/moins/aussi **vite** que les autres athlètes.

Superlative: Superlatif

Definition: The SUPERLATIVE is used when expressing the highest degree of comparison between people and things.

Pierre est **le garçon le plus** attentif_ du groupe.
(Pierre is the most attentive boy of the group.)
Camille est **la fille la moins** attentive du groupe.
(Camille is the least attentive girl of the group.)
Pierre et Luc sont **les garçons les plus** attentifs du groupe.
Camille et Delphine sont **les filles les moins** attentives du groupe.

If the adjective normally precedes the noun, then the superlative precedes the noun as well: (see page 63 for adjectives that preceed the noun)

Delphine est **la plus jeune** musicienne de l'orchestre.
Lucien est **le plus petit** joueur de l'équipe.

Irregular Comparatives and Superlatives

Adjective/Adverb	Comparative	Superlative
bon(s)/bonne(s)	meilleur(s)/meilleure(s)	le/la/les meilleur(e)(s)(es)
bien	mieux	le/la/les mieux
mauvais(e)(es)	plus mauvais(e)(es) pire(s)	le/la/les plus mauvais(e)(es) le/la/les pire(s)
mal	plus mal	le plus mal
petit(e)(s)(es)	plus petit(e)(s)(es) moindre(s)	le/la/les plus petit(e)(s)(es) le/la/les moindre(s)
beaucoup	plus/davantage	le/la/les plus
peu	moins	le/la/les moins

Examples:

Elle est **meilleure** en maths que sa cousine. C'est **la plus mauvaise étudiante** de la classe. Je n'en ai pas **la moindre** idée. C'est **le pire** ennemi des États-Unis. Céline chante **mieux** que Mick. La femme **la mieux habillée** du monde, c'est vous!

1w Indirect Speech: Discours indirect

Direct speech: Il m'a dit: « Vous avez l'air inquiet. »
Indirect speech: Il m'a dit que j'avais l'air inquiet.

Indirect Speech in the Present Tense

In the PRESENT TENSE, the TENSE found between the quotation marks DOES NOT CHANGE.

Paul dit: « Je **sors** avec **ma** copine ce soir. »
Paul dit qu'il **sort** avec **sa** copine ce soir.

Elle me dit: « Tu **as eu** tort de **me** raconter **ton** secret. »
Elle me dit que **j'ai eu** tort de **lui** raconter **mon** secret.

NB | Note how the pronouns and possessive adjectives change accordingly.

Indirect Speech in the Past Tense

In the PAST TENSE, the verbs found between the quotation marks of direct speech will always have the IMPARFAIT/CONDITIONNEL ENDINGS **AIS, AIS, AIT, IONS, IEZ, AIENT** when put into indirect speech.

Présent → Imparfait
Vous avez dit: « Il **fait** très beau à Nice en août. »
Vous avez dit qu'il **faisait** très beau à Nice en août.

Passé Composé → Plus-que-parfait
Il pensait: « Ils **ont gagné** le match sans trop de soucis. »
Il pensait qu'ils **avaient gagné** le match sans trop de soucis.

Futur → Conditionnel présent
Je lui ai dit: « Vous **aurez** de la chance en jouant au loto. »
Je lui ai dit qu'il **aurait** de la chance en jouant au loto.

Futur antérieur → Conditionnel passé
Elle lui a dit: « Vous **serez parti** avant la fin de la séance. »
Elle lui a dit qu'il **serait parti** avant la fin de la séance.

Tenses with the endings ais, ais, ait, ions, iez, aient don't change:
Elle lui a dit: « Tu **t'intéressais** au théâtre quand tu **étais** jeune. »
Elle lui a dit qu'il **s'intéressait** au théâtre quand il **était** jeune.

Ils lui ont dit: « Vous **feriez** mieux de ne pas vous précipiter. »
Ils lui ont dit qu'il **ferait** mieux de ne pas se précipiter.

Indirect Speech with the Interrogative

Il demande: « Les Dupont **seront-ils** ici avant midi? »
Il demande **si** les Dupont seront ici avant midi.

Elle se demande: « **Quand** se mariera-t-il? »
Elle se demande **quand** il se mariera.

Ils ont demandé: « **Pourquoi** étaient-ils en retard? »
Ils ont demandé **pourquoi** ils étaient en retard.

Indirect Speech with the Imperative

Le professeur nous dit: « **Préparez** bien vos exposés pour demain! »
Le professeur nous dit **de** bien préparer nos exposés pour demain!

1
w

1x Passive: Passif

The active voice:	Marc sends the letter.
	(Marc envoie la lettre.)
The passive voice:	The letter is sent by Marc.
	(La lettre **est envoyée par** Marc.)

Verb Structure in the Passive Voice

The passive voice can be used in many different forms. You need to identify the tense that is found in the active voice. Once you have done this, put the verb ÊTRE into the identified tense, then add the PAST PARTICIPLE + PAR (BY).

Remember that in the active voice "Marc sends the letter," Marc is the subject. BUT in the passive voice "The letter is sent by Marc," the letter is the subject. The verb ÊTRE must be conjugated with the subject of the sentence.

ÊTRE in the identified tense + **PAST PARTICIPLE + PAR**.

TENSE	ACTIVE VOICE	PASSIVE VOICE
Present	Marc envoie la lettre.	La lettre **est envoyée par** Marc.
Present perfect	Marc a envoyé la lettre.	La lettre **a été envoyée par** Marc.
Imperfect	Marc envoyait la lettre.	La lettre **était envoyée par** Marc.
Pluperfect	Marc avait envoyé la lettre.	La lettre **avait été envoyée par** Marc.
Future	Marc enverra la lettre.	La lettre **sera envoyée par** Marc.
Near future	Marc va envoyer la lettre.	La lettre **va être envoyée par** Marc.
Future perfect	Marc aura envoyé la lettre.	La lettre **aura été envoyée par** Marc.
Conditional	Marc enverrait la lettre.	La lettre **serait envoyée par** Marc.
Conditional perfect	Marc aurait envoyé la lettre.	La lettre **aurait été envoyée par** Marc.

NB | Don't forget! The past participle must agree with the subject of the sentence:

Le colis a été envoyé_ par Marc.	le colis = masculine singular
La lettre a été envoyée par Marc.	la lettre = feminine singular
Les colis ont été envoyés par Marc.	les colis = masculine plural
Les lettres ont été envoyées par Marc.	les lettres = feminine plural

NB | Two tricks in order to AVOID using the passive:
Instead of saying « La lettre a été envoyée, » you can say, « **On** a envoyé la lettre. »
Instead of saying « Les montres sont vendues ici, » you can say « Les montres **se vendent** ici. »

The Passive Voice with the Construction "To Be Raised by One's Parents":

Être élevé par ses parents

J'**ai** été élevé(**e**)	par mes parents
Tu **as** été élevé(**e**)	par tes parents
Il **a** été élevé_	par ses parents
Elle **a** été élevée	par ses parents
On **a** été élevé(**s**)(**es**)	par ses/nos parents
Nous **avons** été élevés(**es**)	par nos parents
Vous **avez** été élevé(**e**)(**s**)(**es**)	par vos parents
Ils **ont** été élevés	par leurs parents
Elles **ont** été élevées	par leurs parents

1
x

1y Summary–Part 1: Résumé–1re partie

Infinitive: Infinitif

She likes to play the piano. (Elle aime **jouer** du piano.)

Present Tense: Présent

You book a room. / You are booking a room. (Vous **réservez** une chambre.)

Near Future: Futur proche

He is going to buy a new car. (Il **va acheter** une nouvelle voiture.)

Simple Future: Futur simple

I will take the speed train. (Je **prendrai** le TGV.)

Future Perfect: Futur antérieur

I will have achieved my dreams. (J'**aurai réalisé** mes rêves.)

Recent Past: Passé récent

I have just repaired the appliance. (Je **viens de réparer** l'appareil.)

Present Progressive: Présent progressif

I am busy chatting. (Je **suis en train de** bavarder.)

Present Perfect: Passé composé

Amelie considered her options. (Amélie **a considéré** ses options.)

Imperfect: Imparfait

We were speaking to our colleague. (Nous **parlions** à notre collègue.)

Pluperfect: Plus-que-parfait

George had written to his wife. (Georges **avait écrit** à sa femme.)

Imperative: Impératif

Leave immediately! (**Partez** tout de suite!)

Gerund: Gérondif

I fell asleep while reading. (Je me suis endormi **en lisant**.)

Conditional: Conditionnel

She would answer politely if . . . (Elle **répondrait** poliment si...)

Conditional Perfect: Conditionnel passé

He would have come if she had asked. (Il **serait venu** si elle avait demandé.)

Subjunctive: Subjonctif

I want you to come tonight. (Je veux que tu **viennes** ce soir.)

Past Historic: Passé simple

She told the story. (Elle **raconta** l'histoire.)

NB | The PAST HISTORIC is the literary equivalent of the PRESENT PERFECT (PASSÉ COMPOSÉ).

Interrogative: Interrogation

Did you have a nice day? (**Avez-vous passé** une bonne journée?)

Negative: Négation

He doesn't earn a lot of money. (Il **ne** gagne **pas** beaucoup d'argent.)

Passive: Passif

The book was written by Balzac. (Le livre **a été écrit** par Balzac.)

Part 2 Parts of Speech: Parties du discours

2a Tables–Parts of Speech: Tableaux–Parties du discours

Definite and Indefinite Articles:

Definite Articles (the)	Indefinite Articles (a/some)	Noun	Gender and Number
le	un	garçon	masculine singular noun
la	une	fille	feminine singular noun
les	des	garçons	masculine plural noun
les	des	filles	feminine plural noun
l'	un	étudiant	masculine singular noun beginning with a vowel or a mute H
l'	une	étudiante	feminine singular noun beginning with a vowel or a mute H

Possessive Adjectives:

My	Your	His/Her	Our	Your	Their	Noun
mon	ton	son	notre	votre	leur	garçon
ma	ta	sa	notre	votre	leur	fille
mes	tes	ses	nos	vos	leurs	garçons
mes	tes	ses	nos	vos	leurs	filles
mon	ton	son	notre	votre	leur	étudiant
mon	ton	son	notre	votre	leur	étudiante

NB | Notice that ma, ta, sa change to mon, ton, son with a feminine noun that begins with a vowel or a mute H: mon amie, ton attitude, son histoire.

Possessive Pronouns:

Noun	Mine	Yours	His/Hers	Ours	Yours	Theirs
le jardin	le mien	le tien	le sien	le nôtre	le vôtre	le leur
la fleur	la mienne	la tienne	la sienne	la nôtre	la vôtre	la leur
les jardins	les miens	les tiens	les siens	les nôtres	les vôtres	les leurs
les fleurs	les miennes	les tiennes	les siennes	les nôtres	les vôtres	les leurs

Interrogative and Demonstrative Pronouns:

Noun	Interrogative Pronouns (which one)	Demonstrative Pronouns (this one)	Demonstrative Pronouns (that one)
le taxi	lequel	celui-ci	celui-là
la voiture	laquelle	celle-ci	celle-là
les taxis	lesquels	ceux-ci	ceux-là
les voitures	lesquelles	celles-ci	celles-là

Demonstrative, Interrogative and Qualifying Adjectives:

Demonstrative Adjectives (this/these)	Noun	Interrogative Adjectives (what/which)	Noun	Qualifying Adjectives (all the/ the whole	Noun
ce	garçon	quel	garçon	tout le	monde
cette	fille	quelle	fille	toute la	famille
ces	garçons	quels	garçons	tous les	hommes
ces	filles	quelles	filles	toutes les	femmes
cet	étudiant	quel	étudiant		
cette	étudiante	quelle	étudiante		

Contractions of the Definite Article and the Prepositions À and DE:

à + le = **au**	Il va **au** château.
à + la = **à la**	Il va **à la** banque.
à + le/la + vowel/mute h = à l'	Il va **à l'**école.
à + les = **aux**	Il va **aux** cours.

de + le = **du**	Il part **du** château.
de + la = **de la**	Il part **de la** banque.
de + le/la + vowel/mute h = de l'	Il sort **de l'**école.
de + les = **des**	Il revient **des** musées.

2b Definite, Indefinite Articles: Articles définis, Articles indéfinis

Definite Articles: Articles définis

What is a definite article? In English, the DEFINITE ARTICLE is the word THE and it always remains the same. In French, the word THE changes because it must agree in gender and number with the NOUN it qualifies. The word THE in French may take four different forms:

LE = masculine singular
LA = feminine singular
L' = masculine or feminine singular before a vowel or a mute H
LES = masculine or feminine plural

Masculine Singular	Feminine Singular	M. or F. Singular before a vowel/mute H	Masculine or Feminine Plural
le salon	la chambre	l'ami (m.)	les spectacles
le lit	la cuisine	l'infirmière (f.)	les situations
le jardin	la maison	l'histoire (f.)	les escaliers

NB | If the noun begins with an aspirate H, then LE and LA do not become L':
le héros, le hamac, la hache, le haricot, la haine, le hors-d'œuvre.

Indefinite Articles: Articles indéfinis

What is an indefinite article? In English, the INDEFINITE ARTICLES are A, AN and SOME. In French the indefinite article must always agree in gender and in number with the noun it qualifies.

UN = masculine singular
UNE = feminine singular
DES = masculine or feminine plural

Masculine Singular (a/an)	Feminine Singular (a/an)	Masculine or Feminine Plural (some)
un salon	**une** chambre	**des** fauteuils (m.pl.)
un lit	**une** cuisine	**des** chaises (f.pl.)
un jardin	**une** maison	**des** escaliers (m.pl.)

NB The feminine singular UNE is invariable, even when the noun it qualifies begins with a vowel or a mute H: **une** intuition, **une** attitude, **une** exagération, **une** université, **une** histoire, **une** horloge, **une** heure.

NB Remember that the plural of A or AN is SOME: **une** idée → **des** idées, **une** proposition → **des** propositions, **un** sourire → **des** sourires

NB In French the word SOME is used far more frequently than in English:

Vous avez des enfants?   (Do you have children?)
J'ai vu des manifestants dans la rue.   (I saw protestors in the street.)

2
b

2c Partitive: Partitif

Definition: The PARTITIVE simply means SOME. We often omit the word SOME in English when it is INCLUDED and MANDATORY in French. The partitive is used with items that are normally not counted.

Example: I drink wine and beer. = Je bois **du** vin et **de la** bière
(I drink some wine and some beer).

DE + LE = **DU** (some)	Vous avez **du** café, **du** thé ou **du** jus d'orange?
DE + LA = **DE LA** (some)	Elle veut **de la** soupe et **de la** crème fraîche.
DE + LE/LA + VOWEL = **DE L'** (some)	On boit **de l'**eau minérale.
DE + LES = **DES** (some)	Vous avez **des** oranges, **des** bananes et **des** pommes?

The Partitive versus Definite and Indefinite Articles

Il boit **le** café que Julie a préparé.   He drinks the coffee that Julie prepared.
Il boit **un** café.   He drinks a (cup of) coffee.
Il boit **du** café.   He drinks some coffee.

When to Change DU, DE LA, DE L' and DES to DE/D'

1. With Expressions of Quantity:

Beaucoup **de** personnes, un peu **de** communication, assez **d'**ennuis, une bouteille **de** vin, un kilo **de** farine, une centaine **de** livres, une livre **de** fromage.

BUT:
plusieurs erreurs, **quelques** fautes, **la plupart du** temps, **la majorité des** hommes.

2. With a Negative Sentence:

J'ai **du** pain.	Je n'ai pas **de** pain.
Vous avez **de la** classe.	Vous n'avez pas **de** classe.
Nous avons **de l'**argent.	Nous n'avons pas **d'**argent.
Tu as **des** préoccupations.	Tu n'as pas **de** préoccupations.

3. When an Adjective Precedes a Noun in the Plural:

J'ai **un** bon livre.	J'ai **de** bons livres.
Il y a **une** belle peinture ici.	Il y a **de** belles peintures ici.
Vous avez **une** grande armoire.	Vous avez **de** grandes armoires.

BUT:

When an adjective is an integral part of the idea, **DES** remains.

Ex.: **des** jeunes filles, **des** jeunes gens, **des** petits pains, **des** petits pois.

DE, DU, DE LA, DE L' and DES with Possession

Ex.: Sam's toy, his son's toy, etc.

DU, DE LA, DE L', DES	DE	DE
le jouet **du** garcon	le jouet **de** Sam	le jouet **de** son fils
la poupée **de la** fille	la poupée **de** Sylvie	la poupée **de** sa fille
le sac **de l'**étudiant	le sac **de** Fred	le sac **de** mon ami
les idées **des** hommes	les idées **de** Rob et **d'**Yves	les idées **de** nos collègues
les clés **des** femmes	les clés **de** Sue et **de** Kim	les clés **de** vos copines

2d Nouns: Noms

Definition: A NOUN is a word that names a person, an animal, a place, a thing, a condition or a state. Every noun in the French language has a gender. It is either masculine or feminine. If you look up a noun in a French/English dictionary, this is what you will find:

gâteau **n.m.**   =   which stands for **nom masculin** (masculine noun)
baguette **n.f.**   =   which stands for **nom féminin** (feminine noun)

The noun is a very important part of speech because it governs both the gender and number of the words that clarify the noun, known as determiners.

the novels   =   **les** romans   which chairs   =   **quelles** chaises
this letter   =   **cette** lettre   my work   =   **mon** travail
a pretty dress =   **une jolie** robe   all the people =   **tout le** monde

See how the noun governs the gender and the number of its determiners:

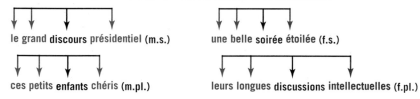

le grand **discours** présidentiel (m.s.)   une belle **soirée** étoilée (f.s.)

ces petits **enfants** chéris (m.pl.)   leurs longues **discussions** intellectuelles (f.pl.)

Nouns also govern the combination À/DE + LE, LA, LES:

Je vais **au** bureau, **à la** boulangerie, **à l'**église et **aux** magasins.
Je viens **du** bureau, **de la** boulangerie, **de l'**église et **des** magasins.

Putting a Noun into the Plural:

Regular nouns	add s	la dame/les dames le détail/les détails
Nouns ending in **au/eau/eu/œu**	add x	le feu/les feux le château/les châteaux
Nouns ending in **al**	change to **aux**	le cheval/les chev**aux** le journal/les journ**aux**
Nouns ending in **ou**	add x	le bijou/les bijoux le caillou/les cailloux
Some nouns ending in **ou**	take s	le clou/les clous le trou/les trous
Nouns ending in s/x/z	stay the same	le prix/les prix le bras/les bras

Some exceptions:
le pneu/les **pneus** le bal/les **bals**
l'œil/les **yeux** le ciel/les **cieux**
le travail/les **travaux** le bail/les **baux**

Gender of Nouns

Nouns ending in **sion/tion/aison/ance/ence/té/ude/ale/ole/ure** are usually feminine:
la traduc**tion**, la renaiss**ance**, la beau**té**, la certit**ude**, la par**ole**, la fact**ure**

Nouns ending in **asme/isme/eau/ment/acle** are usually masculine:
le fant**asme**, le couteau, le chap**eau**, le renseigne**ment**, le spect**acle**

NB | Sometimes the same noun can have a masculine and a feminine form with different meanings:

le livre = book	la livre = pound	le manche = handle	la manche = sleeve
le poste = job	la poste = post office	le tour = stroll/tour	la tour = tower
le vase = vase	la vase = mud	le voile = veil	la voile = sail

2e Adjectives: Adjectifs

Definition: An ADJECTIVE is a word that describes a NOUN or PRONOUN. The ADJECTIVE is usually positioned after the NOUN and agrees with its gender and number.

As a general rule the E feminizes the adjective and the S makes it plural:

Masculine Singular	Masculine Plural
un homme élégant_	des hommes élégants
un livre passionnant_	des films intéressants
un repas parfait_	des comédiens doués

Feminine Singular	Feminine Plural
une femme élégante	des femmes élégantes
une femme intelligente	des voitures vertes
une peinture parisienne	des situations sérieuses

NB | Sometimes the adjective remains the same for both the masculine and the feminine.

Ex.: logique, classique, jeune, facile, difficile, triste, pauvre, rapide, riche, sale, formidable, une journée difficile/un examen difficile, un jeune homme/une jeune femme, le style classique/la musique classique.

Making the Adjective Feminine:

petit/petite, grand/grande, intelligent/intelligente, prêt/prête, vert/verte
cruel/cruelle, ancien/ancienne, pareil/pareille, bas/basse, gros/grosse
flatteur/flatteuse, menteur/menteuse, trompeur/trompeuse
innovateur/innovatrice, créateur/créatrice, admirateur/admiratrice
amoureux/amoureuse, heureux/heureuse, merveilleux/merveilleuse
attentif/attentive, actif/active, destructif/destructive, neuf/neuve
léger/légère, cher/chère, dernier/dernière, complet/complète, fier/fière

Making the Adjective Plural:

petit/petits, grand/grands, intelligent/intelligents, prêt/prêts, vert/verts, noir/noirs
fraîche/fraîches, grosse/grosses, heureuse/heureuses, bonne/bonnes, petite/petites
hébreu/hébreux, beau/beaux, nouveau/nouveaux, cheveu/cheveux, **BUT**: bleu/bleus

NB Some adjectives are invariable: **orange, marron, bleu clair.**
Ex.: Elle a une robe **marron** et des yeux **bleu clair.**

The following adjectives are placed before and not after the noun:

jeune/nouveau	≠ vieux	bon	≠ mauvais
petit	≠ grand/gros	autre	≠ même
court	≠ long/haut	joli/beau ≠	laid/vilain
meilleur	≠ pire		

Examples: un **nouveau** roman, les **jeunes** étudiants, une **petite** poupée,
un **bel** homme, une **jolie** ville

The position of the adjective can change its meaning:

un **cher** ami = a dear friend	une robe **chère** = an expensive dress
un **grand** écrivain = a great writer	un écrivain **grand** = a tall writer
un **pauvre** garçon = a poor boy	un garçon **pauvre** = a poor boy (without money)

Some Common Irregular Adjectives

Masculine Singular	Feminine Singular	Masculine Plural	Feminine Plural
beau but . . . **bel** before a vowel/mute h	belle	beaux	belles
nouveau but . . . **nouvel** before a vowel/mute h	nouvelle	nouveaux	nouvelles
vieux but . . . **vieil** before a vowel/mute h	vieille	vieux	vieilles
doux	douce	doux	douces
fou	folle	fous	folles
long	longue	longs	longues
bref	brève	brefs	brèves
frais	fraîche	frais	fraîches
blanc	blanche	blancs	blanches

2
e

2f Possessive: Possession

Possessive Adjectives: Adjectifs possessifs

Just as the definite articles LE, LA and LES must agree in gender and number with the noun they qualify, the POSSESSIVE ADJECTIVE must do the same:

My	Your	His/Her	Our	Your	Their	Noun
mon	ton	son	notre	votre	leur	garçon
ma	ta	sa	notre	votre	leur	fille
mes	tes	ses	nos	vos	leurs	garçons
mes	tes	ses	nos	vos	leurs	filles
mon	ton	son	notre	votre	leur	étudiant
mon	ton	son	notre	votre	leur	étudiante

NB | Notice that **ma**, **ta**, **sa** change to **mon**, **ton**, **son** with a feminine noun, which begins with a vowel or a mute H. Ex.: **mon** amie, **ton** attitude, **son** histoire.

Possessive Pronouns: Pronoms possessifs

Just as the definite articles LE, LA and LES must agree in gender and number with the noun they qualify, the POSSESSIVE PRONOUN must do the same:

Noun	Mine	Yours	His/Hers	Ours	Yours	Theirs
le jardin	le mien	le tien	le sien	le nôtre	le vôtre	le leur
la fleur	la mienne	la tienne	la sienne	la nôtre	la vôtre	la leur
les jardins	les miens	les tiens	les siens	les nôtres	les vôtres	les leurs
les fleurs	les miennes	les tiennes	les siennes	les nôtres	les vôtres	les leurs

Different Options in Expressing the Possessive

Être à	Appartenir à	Possessive Adjective	Possessive Pronoun
Le livre est à moi/ toi/lui/elle/nous/ vous/eux/elles	Le livre m'appartient/ t'appartient/ lui appartient/ nous/vous/leur appartient	C'est mon/ton/ son/notre/votre/ leur livre	C'est le mien/ le tien/le sien/ le nôtre/le vôtre/ le leur
La clé est à moi/ toi/lui/elle/nous/ vous/eux/elles	La clé m'appartient/ t'appartient/ lui appartient/ nous/vous/leur appartient	C'est ma/ta/sa/ notre/votre/leur clé	C'est la mienne/ la tienne/ la sienne/la nôtre/ la vôtre/la leur
Les livres sont à moi/toi/lui/elle/ nous/vous/eux/ elles	Les livres m'appartiennent/ t'appartiennent/ lui appartiennent/ nous/vous/leur appartiennent	Ce sont mes/tes/ ses/nos/vos/leurs livres	Ce sont les miens/ les tiens/les siens/ les nôtres/ les vôtres/les leurs
Les clés sont à moi/toi/lui/elle/ nous/vous/eux/ elles	Les clés m'appartiennent/ t'appartiennent/ lui appartiennent/ nous/vous/leur appartiennent	Ce sont mes/tes/ ses/nos/vos/leurs clés	Ce sont les miennes/ les tiennes/ les siennes/ les nôtres/ les vôtres/ les leurs

In French there is no apostrophe to indicate possession. So, in order to say the boy's bicycle in French, you have to say "the bicycle of the boy":

Le vélo du garçon.   Le vélo de Robert.   Le vélo de mon garçon.
Le vélo de la fille.   Le vélo de Sylvie.   Le vélo de ma fille.
Les vélos des garçons. Les vélos de Guy et (de) Robert. Les vélos de mes garçons.
Les vélos des filles.   Les vélos de Sylvie et (d')Anne. Les vélos de mes filles.

2g Adverbs: Adverbes

Definition: An ADVERB is a word that modifies a verb, an adjective or another adverb.

Example: Il parle doucement. (He speaks slowly/softly.)

In order to form a REGULAR ADVERB take the ADJECTIVE FINAL, put it into the FEMININE SINGULAR form FINALE and then add "MENT" →
FINALEMENT (finally).

Adjective	Feminine	Adverb
fort	forte	fortement
parfait	parfaite	parfaitement
facile	facile	facilement
rapide	rapide	rapidement
naturel	naturelle	naturellement
heureux	heureuse	heureusement
attentif	attentive	attentivement
sérieux	sérieuse	sérieusement
franc	franche	franchement
complet	complète	complètement
lent	lente	lentement
doux	douce	doucement

Unfortunately there are many irregular adverbs:

hardi → **hardiment**		aveugle → **aveuglément**	
poli → **poliment**		énorme → **énormément**	
vrai → **vraiment**		précis → **précisément**	
absolu → **absolument**		profond → **profondément**	
continu → **continûment**		uniforme → **uniformément**	
abondant → **abondamment**		courant → **couramment**	
évident → **évidemment**		patient → **patiemment**	
gentil → **gentiment**		bref → **brièvement**	

The following adverbs are highly exceptional and very important:

Adjective	Feminine	Adverb
bon	bonne	**bien**
mauvais	mauvaise	**mal**
meilleur	meilleure	**mieux**
petit	petite	**peu**
moindre	moindre	**moins**

Examples:

Elle chante **bien**.

On va **mieux**.

Nous jouons **mal** au tennis.

Il travaille **peu**.

Vous voyez **clairement**.

David se comporte **poliment**.

NB In the present tense, the adverb comes after the verb. But in compound tenses, some adverbs such as **bien, beaucoup, déjà, jamais, mal, mieux, souvent, toujours, trop, vite, bientôt, assez, encore, enfin, moins** are placed between the auxiliary verb and the past participle (usually adverbs of one or two syllables). Adverbs of time like **aujourd'hui, hier, tard, tôt, quelquefois,** etc. are not placed between the auxiliary and the past participle.

Ex.: Nous avons **bien** travaillé. Elle est **déjà** partie. Vous avez **vite** compris.

BUT: Hier, elle est revenue avec son mari. Nous sommes partis **tôt** le matin.

2 g

2h Prepositions: Prépositions

Definition: A PREPOSITION is a word that links a noun, a pronoun or a gerund to other words.

à, au, à la, aux	to, at, in	**sous**	under
après	after	**sur**	on, upon
avant	before (time)	**vers**	toward (direction)
avec	with	**à cause de**	because of
chez	at ___'s house	**à côté de**	beside, next to
contre	against	**afin de**	in order to
dans	in, inside, into	**à travers**	through
de, du, de la, des	of, from	**au-dessus de**	above
depuis	since, for	**au-dessous de**	below
derrière	behind	**au lieu de**	instead of
devant	in front of	**au milieu de**	in the middle of
en	in, to	**auprès de**	close to
entre	between, among	**d'après, selon**	according to
envers	toward	**en dehors de**	outside of
malgré	in spite of	**en dépit de**	in spite of
par	by, through	**en face de**	in front of, facing
parmi	among	**grâce à**	thanks to
pendant	during	**jusqu'à**	until, up to
pour	for, in order to	**loin de**	far from
sans	without	**par rapport à**	with regard to
sauf	except	**près de**	near to
selon	according to	**au moyen de**	by means of

Contraction of the Definite Article and the Prepositions À and DE:

à, au, à la, à l', aux [to the]	de, du, de la, de l', des [from/of the]
Je vais à Paris. [Cities always take à]	Elle arrive de Rome. [Cities always take de/d']
Marie parle au garçon. [à + le = au]	Jean Pierre vient du bureau. [de + le = du]
Les jeunes vont à la fête. [à + la = à la]	Xavier revient de la fête. [de + la = de la]
Ils vont à l'église. [à + le/la + vowel/mute H = à l']	Il parle de l'enfant. [de + le/la + vowel/mute H = de l']
Yves dit bonjour aux élèves. [à + les = aux]	Elle s'occupe des enfants. [de + les = des]

NB | Jean's book, Sylvie's perfume, etc.: le livre de Jean, le parfum de Sylvie, le jouet du garçon, les poupées de la fille, l'atelier de l'artiste, les rôles des comédiens.

Prepositions and Places:

	à (to)	de (from)
With a city:	à Paris, à Milan	de Toulouse, de Londres
With a masculine country:	au Canada, au Japon	du Sénégal, du Portugal
With a feminine country:	en France, en Italie	de Suisse, d'Angleterre
With a plural:	aux États-Unis, aux Antilles	des Pays-Bas, des îles Canaries

NB | All countries ending in E are feminine with the following exceptions: au Mexique, au Cambodge, au Zimbabwe, au Mozambique.

If a masculine country starts with a vowel always use EN: en Israël, en Irak, en Ouganda.

Prepositions and Seasons:

en hiver, en été, en automne, au printemps.

Prepositions and Transport:

à vélo, à pied, à moto, à cheval, en voiture, en autobus, en/par avion, en métro, en taxi, en bateau, en/par le train.

2i Verbs and Their Prepositions: Verbes et leurs prépositions

accepter de faire	descendre du taxi	mériter de
s'adresser à	dire à qqn de faire	se mettre à
s'amuser à	discuter de	se mettre en colère
apprendre à	se diriger vers	mettre en place/œuvre
s'approcher de	douter de	monter dans le taxi
appuyer sur	écrire à qqn	se moquer de
arrêter de	empêcher de	nuire à
arriver à (to succeed)	s'empresser de	s'occuper de
assister à (to attend)	se focaliser sur	ordonner à qqn de
s'attendre à	s'endormir sur	oublier de
avoir confiance en	entrer dans	parler à (speak to)
avoir peur de	essayer de	parler de (speak of)
se battre contre	s'étendre sur	parler pour (speak for)
cesser de	être à	participer à
changer de chemise	être en colère contre	partir dans 10 minutes
chercher à (to try to)	se fâcher contre	partir dans les Alpes
choisir de	faire attention à	partir pour Londres
(re)commencer à	se fier à	parvenir à
compter sur	finir de	se passer de
se concentrer sur	goûter à	payer pour qqn/qqch
conseiller à qqn de	habiter à Paris	penser à (think about)
consentir à	s'habituer à	(se) permettre de
se contenter de	se hâter de	permettre à qqn de
continuer à/de	hésiter à	persister à
convenir à/convenir de	interdire à qqn de	se plaindre à qqn de
croire en Dieu	se jeter sur qqn	se préparer à
décider de	jouer au football	se presser de
se décider à	jouer de la guitare	profiter à (to benefit)
défendre à qqn de	loucher sur	profiter de (to enjoy)
se déguiser en	manger dans l'assiette	promettre à qqn de
demander à qqn de	manquer à (to miss)	proposer à qqn de
se dépêcher de	manquer de (to neglect)	réfléchir à
dépendre de	se marier à	refuser de
(dé)plaire à	se méfier de	se rendre compte de
(dés)obéir à	se mêler à/de	renoncer à

continued

NB qqn = quelqu'un (someone)
qqch = quelque chose (something)

continued

répondre à	aimer qqn	nier qqch
résister à	aller chercher qqn	obtenir qqch
ressembler à	appeler qqn	offrir qqch à qqn
réussir à	approuver qqch	oser faire qqch
rêver à qqn	attendre qqn/qqch	persuader qqn **de**
rêver **de** faire	changer qqch	prêter qqch à qqn
rire **de**	chercher qqn/qqch	pouvoir faire qqch
risquer **de**	commenter qqch	préférer faire qqch
sauter **sur** une occasion	déranger qqn	préférer qqch/qqn à
servir à (to be used for)	descendre la rue	prendre qqch/qqn
se servir **de** (to use)	désirer qqn	prétendre faire qqch
signer **pour** qqn	détester qqn	prier qqn **de** faire
songer à	donner qqch à qqn	questionner qqn **sur**
s'opposer à	échanger qqch **contre**	se rappeler qqch
se soucier **de**	écouter qqn/qqch	regarder qqn/qqch
se souvenir **de**	emmener qqn	regretter qqch
survivre à	emprunter qqch à qqn	rejeter qqn/qqch
tâcher **de**	encourager qqn à	remercier qqn **de** faire
tarder à	ennuyer qqn	remercier qqn **pour**
téléphoner à qqn	envoyer qqch à qqn	savoir qqch
tirer **sur**	épouser qqn	sentir qqch
traduire en (français)	enseigner qqch à qqn	serrer la main à qqn
travailler **pour**	entendre qqn/qqch	soigner qqn/qqch
venir **de** faire qqch	envoyer qqch à qqn	sortir qqch
vivre **dans** le luxe	espérer qqch	souhaiter qqch à qqn
voter **contre**	essayer une robe	subir qqch
voter **pour**	être censé faire qqch	supplier qqn **de**
en vouloir à qqn	féliciter qqn **de**	transformer qqch **en**
BUT:	inviter qqn à faire	troquer qqch **contre**
adorer qqn	interroger qqn **sur**	utiliser qqch
accepter qqch	laisser qqn/qqch	vendre qqch à qqn
acheter qqch à qqn	lire qqch **dans** le journal	voir qqn/qqch
aider qqn à faire qqch	mettre qqch	vouloir qqch

2
i

NB | Elle attend sa copine. | (She is waiting for her friend.)
| Louise cherche son enfant. | (Louise is looking for her child.)
| Elles écoutent la radio. | (They are listening to the radio.)
| Marie-France téléphone à sa mère. | (Marie-France phones her mother.)
| La secrétaire répond à la lettre. | (The secretary answers the letter.)

2j Disjunctive Pronouns: Pronoms toniques

Definition: DISJUNCTIVE PRONOUNS are used to emphasize a noun or a pronoun that refers to a person.

me	moi
you	toi
him	lui
her	elle
one(self)	soi
us	nous
you	vous
them	eux
them	elles

2
j

When to Use the Disjunctive Pronouns

1. After Prepositions:

avec **moi**
sans **toi**
à côté de **lui**
derrière **elle**
chez **soi**
devant **nous**
près de **vous**
selon **eux**
auprès d'**elles**

2. Some expressions take disjunctive pronouns:

	You CAN'T say
Elle s'est moquée de **moi**.	« Elle me s'est moquée. »X
Il faut faire attention à **lui**.	« Il faut lui faire attention. »X
Il s'intéresse à **elle**.	« Il lui s'intéresse. »X
Pierre va vous présenter à **eux**.	« Pierre va vous leur présenter. »X
Vous pensez à **elles**?	« Vous leur pensez. »X
Je tiens beaucoup à **toi**.	« Je te tiens beaucoup. »X

3. With the Expressions "C'EST/CE SONT" and "ÊTRE À" (to Belong to):

C'est toi? Non, **c'est lui**. Mais non, **ce sont eux**.
La montre **est à moi**, mais le bracelet **est à toi**.

4. Comparison:

Elle est plus belle que **toi**.
Vous êtes moins rapide que **moi**.

5. With the Suffix MÊME:

moi-même	myself
toi-même	yourself
lui-même	himself
elle-même	herself
soi-même	oneself
nous-mêmes	ourselves
vous-même(s)	yourself/yourselves
eux-mêmes	themselves
elles-mêmes	themselves

6. Emphasis:

Je vais au spectacle. Et **toi,** tu m'accompagnes? Non! **Moi**, je reste à la maison.

2k Object Pronouns: Pronoms compléments d'objet

Tom writes **the letter.** →
The letter is the DIRECT OBJECT of the verb (no preposition).

Tom talks **TO the child.** →
The child is the INDIRECT OBJECT of the verb (talks to).

Direct Object Pronouns

When the object follows the verb directly and is not separated from it by a preposition, use **LE, LA, L', LES**:

Vous regardez **le match.**	→ Vous **le** regardez.
Je vois **la fille.**	→ Je **la** vois.
Il attend **les copains.**	→ Il **les** attend.
Vous écrivez **les lettres.**	→ Vous **les** écrivez.
Elle invite **Pierre.**	→ Elle **l'**invite.
Tu aides **Stéphanie et Céline.**	→ Tu **les** aides.

Indirect Object Pronouns

When the object is separated by a preposition, use **LUI** (masculine), **LUI** (feminine), **LEUR** (for people/animals):

Elle parle **au garçon.**	→ Elle **lui** parle.
Je téléphone à **ma mère.**	→ Je **lui** téléphone.
Vous demandez **aux employés.**	→ Vous **leur** demandez.
Vous répondez à **Marc et Joanne.**	→ Vous **leur** répondez.

Y

Use **y** for "there" or "to it/to them" (not used for people):

Nous allons **au restaurant.**	→ Nous y allons.
L'assiette est **sur la table.**	→ L'assiette y est.
Elle répond **aux questions.**	→ Elle y répond.

En

Use **en** when the verb is followed by **DE/DU/DE LA/DE L'/DES/QUELQUES** (some/some of it or from it/from them) or with a number/expression of quantity:

Vous avez **de l'argent**?	Oui, j'**en** ai.
Elle s'occupe **de ses affaires**.	Elle s'**en** occupe.
Ils viennent **de Lille**.	Ils **en** viennent.
Vous avez **beaucoup de travail**?	Oui, nous **en** avons beaucoup.
Elle a **des enfants**?	Elle **en** a trois.
Vous avez acheté **combien de pommes**?	J'**en** ai acheté quatre.
J'ai **quelques amies**.	J'**en** ai quelques-unes.

> **NB** ME, TE, NOUS and VOUS can be used as both DIRECT or INDIRECT OBJECT PRONOUNS:
>
> Elle **me** regarde. Elle **te** regarde. Elle **nous** regarde. Elle **vous** regarde.
> In this case **me, te, nous, vous** are DIRECT OBJECT PRONOUNS because the verb REGARDER takes a DIRECT OBJECT. Ex.: Elle regarde **la femme**.
>
> Elle **me** parle. Elle **te** parle. Elle **nous** parle. Elle **vous** parle.
> In this case **me, te, nous, vous** are INDIRECT OBJECT PRONOUNS because the verb PARLER takes an INDIRECT OBJECT. Ex.: Elle parle **à la femme**.

Order of Pronouns When They Precede the Verb:

ME	LE			
TE	LA	LUI		
NOUS	L'	LUI	Y	EN
VOUS	LES	LEUR		

Examples:

Il **me l'**a souvent dit.	Vous **le leur** avez donné.
Je **lui en** ai envoyé.	Il **y en** a tant.

> **NB** With a compound tense the direct or indirect pronoun is placed before the auxiliary verb:
>
> Vous l'avez vu. Elle **lui** aura téléphoné. Nous y étions allés. Je t'aurais reconnu.

2
k

21 Relative Pronouns: Pronoms relatifs

Definition: A RELATIVE PRONOUN is a pronoun, such as "that" or "which," that introduces a relative clause referring to a preceeding word or phrase.

QUE (whom, which, that)

QUE functions as the direct object of a clause and is usually (but not always) followed by a noun or pronoun:

Le restaurant **que vous** aimez n'existe plus.   (Vous aimez **le restaurant**.)
Le tailleur **qu'elle** a acheté est très cher.   (Elle a acheté **le tailleur**.)
Le produit **que la société** propose est de   (La société propose **le produit**.)
très bonne qualité.

NB | que + il/elle = **qu'**il/**qu'**elle, que + ils/elles =**qu'**ils/**qu'**elles

QUI (who, which, that)

QUI functions as the subject of a clause and is usually (but not always) followed by a verb:

La femme **qui parle** est ma soeur.   (**La femme** parle.)
La jeune fille **qui danse** est très jolie.   (**La jeune fille** danse.)
Voyez-vous l'homme **qui donne** le discours?   (**L'homme** donne le discours.)

CE QUI and CE QUE (what–subject/object)

Est-ce que vous comprenez **ce qui** se passe?
(**ce qui** is the subject of the verb "se passe")
Je ne comprends pas **ce que** vous dites!
(**ce que** is the direct object of the verb "dire")

OÙ (where, when)

Le bureau **où** je travaille se trouve loin de chez moi.
C'était l'époque **où** elle était la plus belle.

DONT (whose, of which, about which, of whom, about whom)

If the verb or expression takes DE, then DONT is usually used as the RELATIVE PRONOUN:

Je parle **de la** fille intelligente.	→ La fille **dont** je parle est intelligente.
Le père **du** garçon est avocat.	→ Le garçon **dont** le père est avocat est très ambitieux.
J'admire la beauté **de la** peinture.	→ La peinture **dont** j'admire la beauté est signée Picasso.

Preposition + LEQUEL, LAQUELLE, LESQUELS, LESQUELLES

Le restaurant devant **lequel** j'ai attendu ma copine est excellent.
La maison dans **laquelle** Pierre habite est grande.
Les bâtiments dans **lesquels** vous entrez sont délabrés.
Les raisons pour **lesquelles** j'ai fait cela sont évidentes.

Shortened Forms

à + lequel	= **auquel**	de + lequel	= **duquel**
à + laquelle	= **à laquelle**	de + laquelle	= **de laquelle**
à + lesquels	= **auxquels**	de + lesquels	= **desquels**
à + lesquelles	= **auxquelles**	de + lesquelles	= **desquelles**

Le concert **auquel** il a assisté était formidable.
Les idées **auxquelles** vous faites allusion sont démodées.
Le cœur d'une mère est un abîme au fond **duquel** se trouve toujours un pardon.
(Honoré de Balzac)

QUI Preceded by a Preposition

avec qui:	La femme **avec qui** vous êtes sorti est très belle. (sortir **avec** quelqu'un)
pour qui:	L'économiste **pour qui** j'ai de l'estime s'est trompé. (avoir de l'estime **pour** quelqu'un)
chez qui:	Les gens **chez qui** nous sommes allés sont très gentils. (aller **chez** quelqu'un)

2m Parts of Speech Made Easy:
Parties du discours, simples comme bonjour

PART OF SPEECH	ENGLISH	FRENCH
Definite Article Article défini	the	le, la, l', les
Indefinite Article Article indéfini	a, an, some	un, une, des
Verb Verbe	Robert finds his keys. Jane goes to Avignon.	Robert **trouve** ses clés. Jane **va** à Avignon.
Infinitive of the Verb Infinitif du verbe	to find, to succeed, to learn, to be, to take	**trouver, réussir, apprendre, être, prendre**
Noun Nom	pen, car, sky, love, peace, moon	**stylo, voiture, ciel, amour, paix, lune**
Subject Pronoun Pronom sujet	I, you, he, she, one, we, you, they	**je, tu, il, elle, on, nous, vous, ils/elles**
Adjective Adjectif	pleasant, strong, beautiful, tall, dry, reasonable	**agréable, fort, beau, grand, sec, raisonnable**
Adverb Adverbe	quickly, well, badly, precisely, perfectly	**rapidement, bien, mal, précisément, parfaitement**
Possessive Adjective Adjectif possessif	my, your, his/her/one's, our, your, their	**mon/ma/mes, ton/ta/tes, son/sa/ses, notre/nos, votre/vos, leur/leurs**
Interrogative Adjective Adjectif interrogatif	which	**quel/quelle/quels/ quelles**
Conjunction Conjonction	and, because, but, however	**et, parce que, mais, cependant**

continued

continued

Possessive Pronoun Pronom possessif	mine yours his/hers/one's our's yours theirs	**le mien/la mienne** **les miens/les miennes** **le tien/la tienne** **les tiens/les tiennes** **le sien/la sienne** **les siens/les siennes** **le nôtre/la nôtre/** **les nôtres** **le vôtre/la vôtre/** **les vôtres** **le leur/la leur/les leurs**
Demonstrative Pronoun Pronom démonstratif	this one that one these ones those ones	**celui-ci/celle-ci** **celui-là/celle-là** **ceux-ci/celles-ci** **ceux-là/celles-là**
Demonstrative Adjective Adjectif démonstratif	this these	**ce/cet/cette** **ces**
Preposition Préposition	to, from, with, without, opposite, behind, on	**à, de, avec, sans,** **en face de, derrière, sur**
Partitive Partitif	some	**de, du, de l', de la, des**
Disjunctive Pronoun Pronom tonique	me, you, him, her, one, us, you, them	**moi, toi, lui, elle, soi,** **nous, vous, eux /elles**
Object Pronoun Pronom complément d'objet	I see it/you/her/them I speak to him/her/them	Je **le/te/la/les** vois Je **lui/lui/leur** parle
Relative Pronoun Pronom relatif	I know that you are here The woman who is dancing	Je sais **que** tu es là La femme **qui** danse

Part 3 A Few Very Useful Extras:
Compléments d'informations très utiles

3a Start-Up Vocabulary: Vocabulaire de base

Days of the Week

lundi, mardi, mercredi, jeudi, vendredi, samedi, dimanche
(hier, aujourd'hui, demain, avant-hier, après-demain)

NB | To say every Tuesday or every Friday, simply put the word **le** in front of the day.
| Ex.: Élodie suit des cours de cuisine **le** mardi et **le** vendredi.

Months of the Year

janvier, février, mars, avril, mai, juin, juillet, août, septembre, octobre,
novembre, décembre

NB | Days of the week and months of the year are written in lower case.
| Ex.: Il est parti le **jeudi** 17 février 2008.

Seasons

l'été, l'automne, l'hiver, le printemps
en été, en automne, en hiver, au printemps

Numbers

0–19:	zéro, un, deux, trois, quatre, cinq, six, sept, huit, neuf, dix, onze, douze, treize, quatorze, quinze, seize, dix-sept, dix-huit, dix-neuf
20:	vingt, vingt et un, vingt-deux, vingt-trois
30:	trente, trente et un, trente-deux, trente-trois
40:	quarante, quarante et un, quarante-deux, quarante-trois
50:	cinquante, cinquante et un, cinquante-deux, cinquante-trois
60:	soixante, soixante et un, soixante-deux, soixante-trois
70:	soixante-dix, soixante et onze, soixante-douze, soixante-treize
80:	quatre-vingts, quatre-vingt-un, quatre-vingt-deux
90:	quatre-vingt-dix, quatre-vingt-onze, quatre-vingt-douze
100:	cent, cent un, cent deux, cent trois
500:	cinq cents

continued

continued

1000:	mille (mil)
10 000:	dix mille
1 000 000:	un million (de)
1 000 000 000:	un milliard (de)
1997:	mille (mil) neuf cent quatre-vingt-dix-sept
2010:	deux mille dix

NB In some French speaking countries like Belgium/Switzerland/Democratic Republic of the Congo, the numbers are slightly different and much easier: seventy = **septante**, eighty = **octante** or **huitante**, ninety = **nonante**

NB It is also acceptable to hyphenate all compound numbers: Ex.: cinquante-et-un, mil-neuf-cent-soixante-huit, cent-un

1st, 2nd, 3rd

premier (première), deuxième, troisième, quatrième, cinquième, sixième, septième, huitième, neuvième, dixième, onzième, douzième, treizième, quatorzième, quinzième, seizième, dix-septième, dix-huitième, dix-neuvième, vingtième

About 10, 12, 20, 30, 40, 50, 60, 100

une dizaine de personnes (about ten people), une douzaine, une vingtaine, une trentaine, une quarantaine, une cinquantaine, une soixantaine, une centaine

NB une quinzaine = a fortnight/two weeks

3b Expressions with Être: Expressions avec être

Quel **est** votre nom/prénom?	What is your surname/first name?
Mon nom/prénom **est**…	My surname/first name is …
Être en train de (faire)	To be in the process of (doing)
Être sur le point de (faire)	To be just about to (do)
On **est** quel jour aujourd'hui?	What day is it today?
On **est** vendredi aujourd'hui.	Today is Friday.
Où en **sommes**-nous?	Where are we up to?
Il **était** une fois…	Once upon a time …
Ce livre **est** à moi/toi/lui.	This book belongs to me/you/him.
Elle **est** de New York, il **est** de Paris.	She is from New York, he is from Paris.
Ça m'**est** égal.	I don't mind./It's all the same to me.
Être d'accord	To agree
C'**est** d'accord.	It's all right./Okay.
Être de retour	To be back
Être en retard	To be late
Être en avance	To be early
Être à l'heure	To be on time
Être malade	To be ill
Être prêt	To be ready
Ça y **est**!	There you have it/it's done/that's it!
Être capable de	To be able to
Être au courant de	To be informed/to know about
Est-ce que…/Qu'**est**-ce que…?	Is it that … /What is that … ?
Qui **est**-ce?	Who is it?
N'**est**-ce pas?	Isn't it?
C'**est**/Ce **sont**	It is/These are
Ainsi **soit**-il!	So be it!
Peut-**être**	Maybe
Être pressé	To be in a hurry

Le bien être	Well-being
Être de bonne humeur	To be in a good mood
Être de mauvaise humeur	To be in a bad mood
Être à bout de forces	To have no strength left
Être à bout de souffle	To be out of breath
Être à l'aise	To be at ease
Être mal à l'aise	To be ill at ease
Être facile à faire	To be easy to do
Être de mise	To be acceptable
Être en mesure de faire qqch	To be able to do something
Être à même de faire qqch	To be able to do something
Être difficile à vivre	To be difficult to get along with
Être de mèche avec qqn	To be in cahoots with someone
Être dans le pétrin	To be in a jam
Être dans le brouillard	To be clueless
Être dans le besoin	To be in need
Je suis dans l'informatique.	I'm in computing.
Je ne suis pas très pizza.	I don't really like pizza.

Quelle heure est-il?

What time is it?

Il est une heure.	It's one o'clock.
Il est deux/trois/quatre heures.	It's two/three/four o'clock.
Il est cinq heures cinq/dix/vingt.	It's five/ten/twenty past five.
Il est six heures et quart.	It's a quarter past six.
Il est sept heures et demie.	It's half past seven.
Il est huit heures moins cinq/dix/vingt.	It's five/ten/twenty to eight.
Il est neuf heures moins le quart.	It's a quarter to nine.
Il est midi/minuit.	It's noon/midnight.
Il est midi vingt.	It's twenty past twelve. (day)
Il est minuit moins cinq.	It's five to twelve. (night)
Il est dix-neuf heures quarante-cinq.	It's 7:45 p.m.

3c Expressions with Avoir: Expressions avec avoir

There are many expressions in French where avoir **means to be!**

Avoir chaud	To be hot
Avoir froid	To be cold
Avoir faim	To be hungry
Avoir soif	To be thirsty
Avoir sommeil	To be sleepy
Avoir peur de	To be afraid of
Avoir honte de	To be ashamed of
Avoir raison	To be right
Avoir tort	To be wrong
Avoir mal à la jambe/au genou	To have a sore leg/knee
Avoir lieu	To happen/occur
Avoir l'air	To seem
Avoir de la chance	To be lucky
Avoir de la patience	To have patience
Avoir 10 minutes de retard	To be 10 minutes late
Avoir 10 minutes d'avance	To be 10 minutes early
Avoir envie de	To feel like
Avoir besoin de	To need
Avoir l'habitude de	To have the habit of
Avoir l'occasion de	To have the opportunity of
Avoir l'intention de	To have the intention of
Avoir le temps de	To have the time to
Avoir quelque chose	To have something wrong
Qu'est-ce que tu **as?**	What's the matter?
Avoir 25 ans	To be 25 years old
Avoir dix mètres de longueur/largeur	To be ten metres long/wide
Avoir à…	To have to
J'**ai** à travailler.	I have to work.
Il y **a**	There is/There are
Il y **a eu**	There was/There were

Il y **avait**	There was/There were
Il va y **avoir**	There is/are going to be
Il y **aura**	There will be
Il y **aurait**	There would be
Il y **a** trois mois	Three months ago
Se faire **avoir**	To be had
Je me suis fait **avoir**!	I've been had!
En **avoir** marre	To be fed up
En **avoir** ras le bol	To be sick to death
Avoir la pêche	To be full of get-up-and-go
Avoir accès à	To have access to
Avoir des doutes	To have doubts
Avoir du mal à faire qqch	To have difficulty doing something
Avoir la tête qui tourne	To be dizzy
Avoir le trac	To have stage fright
Avoir le fou rire	To have the giggles
Avoir le coeur gros	To feel sad
Avoir le cafard	To be down in the dumps
Avoir la trouille	To be scared to death
Avoir la tête dans les nuages	To have one's head in the clouds
Avoir un petit creux	To feel peckish, a little hungry
Avoir un trou de mémoire	To have a lapse in memory
Avoir le moral à zero	To feel down
Avoir le mal de mer	To be seasick
Avoir le mal du pays	To be homesick

NB "Il me faut…" is another way of saying: J'**ai** besoin de (I need).
Ex.: Il me faut huit heures de sommeil. (I need eight hours sleep.)
J'**ai** besoin de huit heures de sommeil. (I need eight hours sleep.)

3
c

3d Expressions with Faire: Expressions avec faire

Ça/Cela **fait** combien?	How much is it?
Comment ça se **fait** qu'il parle russe?	How is it that he speaks Russian?
Ça ne se **fait** pas.	One doesn't do (this type of thing).
Il faut **faire** avec.	One must learn to live with it.
Ne t'en **fais** pas./Ne vous en **faites** pas!	Don't worry about it!
Il faut s'y **faire**.	One must get used to it.
Je me suis **fait** couper les cheveux.	I had my hair cut.
Elle lui a **fait** porter sa valise.	She had him carry her suitcase.
Il **fait** jour/nuit.	It's day/night.
Ça ne **fait** rien.	It doesn't matter.
Faire l'impossible	To do the impossible
Faire de son mieux pour	To do one's best in order to
Ça me **fait** du bien.	It's good for me.
Faire fortune	To make a fortune
Faire des économies	To save money
Faire mal/Ça me fait mal!	To hurt/It hurts!
Se **faire** mal au genou	To hurt one's knee
Faire attention à	To be careful of
Faire peur à	To scare
Faire confiance à	To trust
Faire la connaissance de quelqu'un	To make someone's acquaintance
Faire les courses	To do the shopping
Faire le ménage	To do the housework
Faire la cuisine	To cook
Faire la lessive	To do the washing
Faire la vaisselle	To wash the dishes
Faire les devoirs	To do homework
Faire sa toilette	To wash oneself
Faire du sport	To do sport
Faire du vélo	To ride a bicycle
Faire de la musique	To make music
Faire du théâtre	To do drama
Faire du jogging/footing	To jog
Faire la queue	To stand in line

3
d

Faire un voyage	To go on a trip
Faire une promenade	To go for a walk
Faire quelque chose exprès	To do something on purpose
Faire semblant de	To pretend to
Faire plaisir à	To please
Faire des études (en droit)	To study (law)
Faire les valises	To pack your suitcase
Vous **faites** quelle taille/pointure?	What's your clothing/shoe size?
Je **fais** du 34./Je fais du 8.	I'm a size 34./I'm a size 8.
Je **fais** lm82.	I'm six feet tall.
Je **fais** 80 kilos.	I'm 175 pounds.

Quel temps fait-il?

What's the weather like?

Il **fait** beau.	The weather is nice.
Il **fait** mauvais.	The weather is bad.
Il **fait** chaud.	It's hot.
Il **fait** froid.	It's cold.
Il **fait** frais.	It's cool.
Il **fait** du soleil.	It's sunny.
Il **fait** du vent.	It's windy.
Il **fait** du brouillard.	It's foggy.
Il **fait** une chaleur torride.	It's a scorcher.

3
d

3e Extremely Useful Expressions: Expressions extrêmement utiles

Être en train de + (inf.)	To be in the process of
Venir de + (inf.)	To have just
Être sur le point de + (inf.)	To be about to
Avoir besoin de	To need
Avoir envie de	To feel like
Avoir l'air	To seem
Il y a	There is/are
Il y a deux mois	Two months ago
Il s'agit de	It's about
S'occuper de	To take care of
Avoir lieu	To take place
S'intéresser à	To be interested in
Il faut (que)	One must
Il est nécessaire (de/que)	It is necessary (to/that)
Mettre du temps à faire qqch	To take time to do something
S'en aller	To be off
En vouloir à quelqu'un	To hold something against someone
Être à quelqu'un	To belong to someone
Croire que/Penser que	To think that
Se tromper	To be mistaken
Suivre des cours	To take lessons
Faire du mal à quelqu'un	To hurt someone
Faire plaisir à quelqu'un	To please
Se débrouiller	To get by/to manage
C'est-à-dire	In other words
Ça y est, on y va!	That's it, let's go!
Mettre l'accent sur/souligner	To emphasize
Se concentrer sur	To focus on
Faites-moi confiance!	Trust me!
Je suis marié depuis 5 ans.	I have been married for 5 years.
C'est hallucinant/scandaleux.	It's unbelievable/outrageous.
Laissez-moi tranquille!	Leave me alone!

Installez-vous!/Asseyez-vous!	Sit down.
Je vous en prie./Je t'en prie.	It's a pleasure.
Ça te plaît? Oui, ça me plaît.	Do you like it? Yes, I do.
Il faut en profiter.	You must enjoy it.
C'est parti!	Off we go!
Quand même	Nevertheless
Tant pis	Too bad
Tant mieux	All the better
Se moquer de	To make fun of
Tomber en panne	To break down (car/machine/appliance)
Se trouver	To be situated (somewhere)
La poste se trouve en face du bar.	The post office is opposite the bar.
Prendre rendez-vous	To make an appointment
Partir en vacances	To go on vacation
Prendre un café	To have a cup of coffee
Offrir un cadeau	To give a gift
Gagner du temps	To save time
Perdre du temps	To waste time
Présenter qqn	To introduce someone
Proposer qqch	To suggest something
Se servir de	To use
Donner des cours	To give lessons/To teach
S'en prendre à qqn	To take it out on someone
S'y prendre	To set about (doing) it
S'y connaitre en qqch	To be well versed in something
Se mettre à faire qqch	To start doing something
Arriver à faire qqch	To manage to do something
Je vous dois combien?	How much do I owe you?
On prend un verre ensemble?	Shall we have a drink together?
Bravo!/Chapeau!	Well done!
À la vôtre!/À la tienne!	Cheers!
Impéccable!	Great!

3
e

3f French Accents, Aspirate H: Accents français, H aspiré

French Accents: Accents français

L'accent aigu é

la secrétaire, la télévision, j'ai discuté, l'équipe.
The acute accent is by far the most common accent in French.

L'accent grave è

j'achète, les élèves, complète, l'étrangère, la mère, très, après.
The grave accent is the second most common accent and usually occurs at the end of a word when you have the combination E + CONSONANT + E(S): LE PÈRE, LES FRÈRES, TU ACHÈTES. Remember that the accent grave is also found on the À: il **a** (he has), **BUT:** Il va à Londres. (He goes to London.)

L'accent circonflexe ê

le rêve, je suis prêt, vous êtes sûr, j'ai dû, l'hôtel, l'hôpital.
As you learn the language you will come to recognize the words that take the accent circonflexe. It is often included when the word has lost a letter over time: HOSPITAL–HÔPITAL, HOSTEL–HÔTEL.

La cédille ç

le garçon, le français, François, nous commençons, ça va?
The cédille softens the C and makes it an S sound. If the C is followed by an **E, I** or **Y** it keeps the S sound: cesser, certain, circulation, ciel, cycle. BUT if it is followed by an **O, A** or **U**, the C sound remains: comment, cadeau, culpabilité. Let's take the word **CICATRICE** for example. The first C has an S sound, the second C keeps the C sound and the third C has the S sound once again: CICATRICE is pronounced SIKATRIS!

Le tréma ü, ë, ï

aiguë, ambiguë, coïncider, maïs, ouïe.
The tréma tells us to pronounce the preceding vowel separately.

NB | It is correct to use accents with CAPITAL LETTERS, but they are sometimes omitted.

Aspirate H: H aspiré

There are two types of **H** in French: the MUTE H which is more common and has the SAME VALUE as a VOWEL: L'HÔPITAL, L'HÔTEL, L'HOMME, L'HUMANITÉ and the ASPIRATE H which has the value of a CONSONANT: LE HÉROS, LA HAINE, JE HURLE. Here are some common French words with the ASPIRATE H. Remember that the letter **H** is never pronounced.

la hache (axe)	**la hausse** (rise/increase)
la haie (hedge/hurdle)	**le haut** (top)
la haine (hatred)	**hautain** (haughty/lofty)
haïr (to hate)	**la havane** (Havana tobacco)
le hall (lobby)	**le havre** (haven)
la halle (market/hall)	**le héron** (heron)
la halte (pause/break)	**le héros** (hero)
le hamac (hammock)	**le hibou** (owl)
le hamster (hamster)	**le hockey** (hockey)
la hanche (hip)	**la Hollande** (Holland)
le hand-ball (handball)	**le homard** (lobster)
le hangar (hangar/shed)	**la Hongrie** (Hungary)
hanter (to haunt)	**la honte** (shame)
harceler (to harass)	**le hoquet** (hiccup)
le harem (harem)	**hors** (outside)
le hareng (herring)	**la housse** (protective cover)
le harnais (harness)	**le hublot** (porthole)
la harpe (harp)	**à huis clos** (behind closed doors)
le harpon (harpoon)	**le huit** (eight)
le hasard (chance/fate)	**hurler** (to scream/yell)
le hachisch (hashish)	**le Huron** (Lake Huron)
la hâte (haste)	**la hutte** (hut)

3
f

NB | When you have a MUTE H, make the liaison LES_HOMMES, but when you have an ASPIRATE H, then there is no liaison: LES HOMARDS.

3g Useful Irregular Verbs (Cont.): Verbes irréguliers utiles (suite)

Accueillir (to welcome) J'accueille Tu accueilles Il/Elle/On accueille Nous accueillons Vous accueillez Ils/Elles accueillent	**Apercevoir** (to notice) J'aperçois Tu aperçois Il/Elle/On aperçoit Nous apercevons Vous apercevez Ils/Elles aperçoivent	**Appartenir** (to belong) J'appartiens Tu appartiens Il/Elle/On appartient Nous appartenons Vous appartenez Ils/Elles appartiennent
S'asseoir (to sit) Je m'assieds Tu t'assieds Il/Elle/On s'assied Nous nous asseyons Vous vous asseyez Ils/Elles s'asseyent	**Atteindre** (to reach) J'atteins Tu atteins Il/Elle/On atteint Nous atteignons Vous atteignez Ils/Elles atteignent	**Battre** (to beat) Je bats Tu bats Il/Elle/On bat Nous battons Vous battez Ils/Elles battent
Conduire (to drive) Je conduis Tu conduis Il/Elle/On conduit Nous conduisons Vous conduisez Ils/Elles conduisent	**Construire** (to construct) Je construis Tu construis Il/Elle/On construit Nous construisons Vous construisez Ils/Elles construisent	**Courir** (to run) Je cours Tu cours Il/Elle/On court Nous courons Vous courez Ils/Elles courent
Craindre (to fear) Je crains Tu crains Il/Elle/On craint Nous craignons Vous craignez Ils/Elles craignent	**Décevoir** (to disappoint) Je déçois Tu déçois Il/Elle/On déçoit Nous décevons Vous décevez Ils/Elles déçoivent	**Disparaître** (to disappear) Je disparais Tu disparais Il/Elle/On disparaît Nous disparaissons Vous disparaissez Ils/Elles disparaissent
Éteindre (to extinguish) J'éteins Tu éteins Il/Elle/On éteint Nous éteignons Vous éteignez Ils/Elles éteignent	**Fuir** (to flee) Je fuis Tu fuis Il/Elle/On fuit Nous fuyons Vous fuyez Ils/Elles fuient	**Inclure** (to include) J'inclus Tu inclus Il/Elle/On inclut Nous incluons Vous incluez Ils/Elles incluent

continued

continued

Inscrire (to enrol)	Joindre (to join)	Mentir (to lie)
J'inscris	Je joins	Je mens
Tu inscris	Tu joins	Tu mens
Il/Elle/On inscrit	Il/Elle/On joint	Il/Elle/On ment
Nous inscrivons	Nous joignons	Nous mentons
Vous inscrivez	Vous joignez	Vous mentez
Ils/Elles inscrivent	Ils/Elles joignent	Ils/Elles mentent
Mourir (to die)	Naître (to be born)	Offrir (to offer)
Je meurs	Je nais	J'offre
Tu meurs	Tu nais	Tu offres
Il/Elle/On meurt	Il/Elle/On naît	Il/Elle/On offre
Nous mourons	Nous naissons	Nous offrons
Vous mourez	Vous naissez	Vous offrez
Ils/Elles meurent	Ils/Elles naissent	Ils/Elles offrent
Peindre (to paint)	Prévoir (to forecast)	Produire (to produce)
Je peins	Je prévois	Je produis
Tu peins	Tu prévois	Tu produis
Il/Elle/On peint	Il/Elle/On prévoit	Il/Elle/On produit
Nous peignons	Nous prévoyons	Nous produisons
Vous peignez	Vous prévoyez	Vous produisez
Ils/Elles peignent	Ils/Elles prévoient	Ils/Elles produisent
Recevoir (to receive)	Reconnaître (to recognize)	Sentir (to smell)
Je reçois	Je reconnais	Je sens
Tu reçois	Tu reconnais	Tu sens
Il/Elle/On reçoit	Il/Elle/On reconnaît	Il/Elle/On sent
Nous recevons	Nous reconnaissons	Nous sentons
Vous recevez	Vous reconnaissez	Vous sentez
Ils/Elles reçoivent	Ils/Elles reconnaissent	Ils/Elles sentent
Servir (to serve)	Traduire (to translate)	Valoir (to be worth)
Je sers	Je traduis	Je vaux
Tu sers	Tu traduis	Tu vaux
Il/Elle/On sert	Il/Elle/On traduit	Il/Elle/On vaut
Nous servons	Nous traduisons	Nous valons
Vous servez	Vous traduisez	Vous valez
Ils/Elles servent	Ils/Elles traduisent	Ils/Elles valent

3
g

Index: Index